JOINING THE MILITARY

A McFarland Handbook Series
by Snow Wildsmith

Joining the United States Air Force

A *Handbook*

SNOW WILDSMITH

JOINING THE MILITARY, 1

McFarland & Company, Inc., Publishers
Jefferson, North Carolina, and London

LIBRARY OF CONGRESS CATALOGUING-IN-PUBLICATION DATA

Wildsmith, Snow, 1973–
Joining the United States Air Force : a handbook / Snow Wildsmith.
p.   cm. — (Joining the military ; 1)
Includes bibliographical references and index.

ISBN 978-0-7864-4758-9
softcover : acid free paper ∞

1. United States. Air Force — Vocational guidance.   I. Title.
UG633.W567 2012   358.40023'73 — dc23   2012010677

BRITISH LIBRARY CATALOGUING DATA ARE AVAILABLE

On the cover: *inset* seal of the United States Air Force; *photograph* the
Thunderbirds fly over as 1001 U.S. Air Force Academy cadets are
commissioned second lieutenants at the close of the class of 2010 graduation
ceremony, May 26, 2010, at the United States Air Force Academy, Colorado
(United States Air Force photograph/Mike Kaplan)

Manufactured in the United States of America

*McFarland & Company, Inc., Publishers
Box 611, Jefferson, North Carolina 28640
www.mcfarlandpub.com*

For my father,
HMCM Donald P. Wildsmith, USN (Ret.),
with love and respect for all he has given
for me and for his country.

Acknowledgments

This book could not have been written without the support of the United States Air Force. Thank you to all of the airmen who took the time out of their busy days to answer my questions, supply me with needed information, tour me around recruit training, and generally help me out with whatever I needed.

Thank you also to librarian and friend Emily Leachman for proofreading my rough drafts and making suggestions for improvement. I owe a debt of gratitude to all of my friends and family who supported me during the writing process, especially to my ever-patient and ever-loving husband Barry.

Table of Contents

Read This First

Patriotism. Money for college. Family tradition. Job training. Adventure. Secure employment. Travel. Service to others. The opportunity to do something different. There are as many reasons to join the military as there are people in the military. Some people want to make a full career out of their military service. Some just want to get in, do their time, and get the benefits they've earned. Others are in the middle — they aren't sure where they want to go after the military or how long they want to spend in the service, but they think it might be a good job for the time being.

Whether you are certain that you want to enter the military or you are just curious and want more information, you still will need to consider a lot of factors before you join. This series of books is designed to help you look at all of your options to see whether or not military service is right for you and, if so, to help you figure out which branch of the service is for you. There is one book for each branch of the service: Air Force, Army, Coast Guard, Marine Corps, and Navy. Within each book, there are sections on:

- Looking at your personality to see if you will fit the military lifestyle
- Talking with a recruiter to find out what the service offers and what they expect from you in return
- How enlisting works and what you need to do during the process
- Taking the Armed Services Vocational Aptitude Battery test
- Preparing for recruit training (also called basic training) mentally, physically, emotionally, and socially

- What happens during basic training
- Books, DVDs, and websites with more information on joining the military, military history, and life in the military

Joining the military is a major lifestyle change, one which will affect not only you, but also your family and your friends. You'll need to think long and hard about all of your options and the choice you are about to make. These books will give you the basic information you need, but you should know that every individual's enlistment and training experience is different, shaped by their personality, education, goals, and interests. Additionally, the branches of the military are constantly evaluating and adjusting their policies and procedures to meet their current needs. The military personnel you speak with during your time considering military service will have up-to-date information about enlistment and training.

Whatever branch you choose to serve in, however long your term of enlistment, whichever occupational specialty you pick — you will be part of something larger than you. Deciding to become a serviceman or servicewoman can be the best thing that ever happened to you as it guides the rest of your life in ways you never expected.

ONE

Thinking About Joining the Military

Things to Consider
for Potential Enlistees

There are many big decisions people make over their lifetime. "Should I go to college or get a job?" "Who will I marry?" "Will I have children?" "Where will I live?" Deciding to join the military is one of those momentous decisions. If you decide to join, you will be committing yourself to service to the government for at least eight years — the length of your active duty contract plus the years you are obligated to spend in the Individual Ready Reserve, where you aren't actively doing military training and work, but can still be called up by the government. Because you will be making a legal, binding contract that cannot be gotten out of easily, you must consider all of the factors carefully before deciding to enlist in the military. Take your time, do your research, and, most of all, don't let anyone pressure you to join or not to join. This is your life and the decision should be yours.

Pros and Cons

The first thing to consider are the positives and negatives of joining the military — the pros and cons. What will you gain by joining and what will you have to sacrifice?

Pros

- Employment — joining the military will give you a job with a steady, guaranteed income as well as health insurance, housing, and a clothing allowance

- Training — the military offers training on a wide variety of jobs, and you will be paid, fed, clothed, and housed while you are training
- Education — in addition to the job training offered by the military, you will also earn money to help pay for future education; you can even start college and earn a degree while serving in the military — sometimes completely paid for by the military
- Travel — service in the military pretty much guarantees travel, both in the U.S. and around the world
- Purpose — military service is just that: service; you will be serving your country and working for something bigger than just you

CONS

- War — the first and most important job of the military is to protect the United States; by joining you face the very real possibility of ending up in a war zone
- Freedom — by joining the military you will be voluntarily giving up a good amount of your personal freedom for the regimen of military life
- Time — serving in the military means a lot of hard work, often including long hours and even days, weeks, or months away from friends and family
- Training and Education — there are a lot of training and education opportunities in the military, but the military's interest is to train you in what they need to you do, so your education desires come second if they don't fit with current military needs
- Travel — you will travel and you will have some say in where you travel to, but not always; if some get to serve in Paris or Hawaii, many serve in much less glamorous locales

These are some of the major factors to consider as you begin to think about possible military service. As you learn more about the military, you'll also need to consider whether or not you are a good candidate for the military and whether or not the military can help you achieve the goals you have set for your life.

Your Personality, Your Goals, and Your Future Aspirations

The military has its own goals and its own direction for the future and so should you. It is important that you think about what your goals are before deciding if military service is right for you. If you don't have goals planned out, now is the time to make them. Start thinking about what you might want to accomplish in the future. The military will be happy to use your hard work to accomplish its goals, but if its goals are not the same as what you want to do with your life, then your time of service will be one of frustration.

Additionally, you should think about the military lifestyle and whether or not it fits with your personality. The military is regimented, ordered, and focused on teamwork. If you are a rugged individualist, then military service might not be an easy job for you as your superiors will try to change that mindset.

This book and the others in this series focus on enlisted careers in the military. "Enlisted" means those servicemen and women who are not officers. Enlisted personnel are responsible for the daily operations of the military, whereas officers are the command personnel, the ones who give the orders. That doesn't mean that enlisted service members don't lead. There are a lot of opportunities for enlisted men and women to learn and practice leadership skills, starting as early as basic training. The higher ranks of enlisted personnel are called "non-commissioned officers" and they take on many of the leadership roles in the military. You do not need a college degree to enlist in the military, but you do need one to be commissioned — meaning appointed — as an officer. That is another factor to keep in mind as you are deciding if a military career is right for you.

MILITARY QUESTIONNAIRE

The following questionnaire will help you think about your lifestyle, your personality, and your future to see if they might fit well with the military.

Read each statement and see if "yes"—it does agree with you, "no"—it does not agree with you, or "maybe"—it sort of agrees with you or you aren't sure. There are no right or wrong answers. These are just factors to consider. The notes after each statement will help you see how that statement does or does not fit with a possible career in the military.

YES   NO   MAYBE   I am interested in serving in the military because of patriotic reasons.

- This is a great reason to join the military. Having a high degree of patriotism means that you'd be willing to offer up your life to protect and serve your country. But there are other ways that patriotic people can serve the United States, so if you aren't certain that military service is for you, consider non-military service options.

YES   NO   MAYBE   I am interested in serving in the military because I want to give back to others.

- Also a good reason to join the military, but again, if you are positive that you wish to serve others, but uncertain about the military, there are other options that will allow you to help out.

YES   NO   MAYBE   I am interested in serving in the military because my father/mother/other family member served.

- This is another good reason for joining. If you were raised in a military family or if you grew up hearing stories about a family member's military service, then you will probably be proud to serve and carry on a family tradition. Make sure, though, that you get the most recent information on military life and make sure that your personality and goals are as compatible with military service as your family member's were. Also be sure that you are not joining because....

YES   NO   MAYBE   My father/mother/other family member says that I have to join the military.

- DO NOT allow yourself to be forced or coerced into military

8

A new Airman hugs her mother, an Air Force Master Sergeant (Official U.S. Air Force photograph by Staff Sgt. Vernon Young, Jr.).

service. It is your life and your decision. No one else can make it for you.

YES   NO   MAYBE   I want to serve in the military, but only part-time, and/or I don't want to have to move away from where I am living.

- Then you will want to consider enlisting as a reservist. Service men and women in the reserves serve one weekend a month and two weeks out of the year, during which time they train with a local unit. Reservists are still members of the military and are subject to the same regulations and laws as active duty service members, as well as receiving many of the same benefits that active-duty personnel receive. You should know, however, that as a reservist you can be called up to active duty for a period of time ranging from several weeks to several years in order to fight in war. And job choices in the reserves can be limited, as they are almost always assigned based on the needs of the reserve unit with which you will serve.

YES   NO   MAYBE   I want to serve in the military, but only for my initial term of enlistment (usually four years).

- It is possible to sign up for a four year stint in the military, complete your time, and then choose not to reenlist. However, there are some factors to keep in mind. First of all, even after you finish your term and leave the military, you are still part of the military until you have completed a full eight years of service. The enlistment contract that you sign when you join the military makes it clear that you are obligated for those eight years and that any time you don't spend as active duty must be spent in the inactive reserves, called the Individual Ready Reserve (IRR). While you are in the IRR, you can still be called up to duty if the military needs you.

- If the military still needs your services at the end of your enlistment term, it can prevent you from leaving. A program called "Stop Loss" allows the military, during times of conflict, to prevent you for up to one year from leaving at your normal separation date. The military has been using this program during the conflicts in Iraq and Afghanistan to ensure that personnel who are doing specific jobs are still around to do those jobs when the military needs them.

YES   NO   MAYBE   I have dropped out of or not finished high school or I have my GED or I am considering dropping out of high school.

- Today's military wants service members who have at least finished high school. If you are still in school, you will need to finish and graduate, trying for the best grades you can get. If you have dropped out, you will have to get a GED in order to be eligible to enlist. However, every branch of the military has strict limitations on how many people they will accept with GEDs each year and those candidates must score higher grades on the Armed Services Vocational Aptitude Battery (ASVAB) test which all potential enlistees must take. (More on the

ASVAB in Part Three.) Your best bet is to get your GED and also have at least 15 hours of college credit. With most branches of the military, that will put you on the same footing as a high school graduate.

YES NO MAYBE   I am interested in serving in the military because I have nothing better to do with my life.

- On the one hand, this is a terrible reason for joining the military. You need to think a lot more about what you are capable of and where you see yourself in the future. Joining the military should not be a spur of the moment decision or one made because you are bored or directionless. You must carefully consider all aspects of an enlistment decision and look for all options available to you, even if you aren't sure right now what those options are. Careful research will help you make the right choice for your future.

- On the other hand, the military is willing to take your raw material and mold you into the warrior it needs. If you are open to allowing yourself to be guided, the military can help you find a job and training while you figure out who you are and what you want out of life. Just be sure that you are willing to give them eight years of your life to do it.

YES NO MAYBE   I am interested in serving in the military for the education benefits: money for college.

- Money is available for those who have served in the military and who now want to attend college. Make sure that you get information on how long you'll need to serve, what types of service are eligible, how much money you'll receive, and how and when that money can be used in the future. The next chapter offers information on the benefits of enlisting, including education benefits, and military recruiters will always be able to give you the most up-to-date information available. (More on talking to recruiters in Part Three.)

YES   NO   MAYBE   I am interested in serving in the military for the job benefits: training, housing, etc.

- The military is a great way to learn a career and get paid while you're learning. Remember, though, that the military's selection of jobs in the fields which interest you may be limited and/or the military may or may not find you qualified for training in the job you want. If you can't get the training that you're interested in, you can see if the military offers another job which you would be interested in doing or you will have to look for civilian training in the career you want.

YES   NO   MAYBE   I have computer, mechanical, scientific, medical, administrative, or technical interests or skills that I want to make into a career and need to be trained in.

- These are great skills to hone in the military, though if you aren't planning on making the military a life-long career, then you will want to look for a military job which will allow you to learn skills that you can use in civilian life after your term of service is up. Check out one of the books or websites on military jobs in the appendix under "For More Information—Career Planning." They will help give you an idea of what military jobs are available and how they correspond to civilian work.

YES   NO   MAYBE   I have artistic interests or skills that I want to make into a career and need training in.

- Many people assume that the military only offers technical jobs, but if you want a more artistic career, the military has jobs for you as well. There are some spots for chefs, musicians, graphic designers, and more in the military, but the number of these jobs available can be lower than other positions, so competition is often higher.
- If you are willing to delay your artistic career in favor of serving in the military, you can choose a different career path during your service and then use your educational benefits to study your art once you have left or retired from the military.

YES   NO   MAYBE   I want a job that can become a lifetime career.
- The military is a good possibility for a lifetime career. As long as you are willing to apply yourself to your work, you can retire after 20 or 30 years and still be young enough to enjoy yourself and even start a second career while also collecting your military retirement pay.

YES   NO   MAYBE   I need a job for now, but I am not sure that I want to make a life-long commitment.
- The military is also a great choice for those who want a job for now, but who aren't sure that they want to stay in that career forever. You'll have the opportunity to reenlist every few years and can decide at that time if you want to stay in or get out. If you decide to stay in, though, you're bound for the next few years, so the military is not a good choice for those who like to switch jobs every year. Consider what job you want to do and think about if you'll want to do it in the military for at least two, four, or six years, depending on how long your term of enlistment is.

YES   NO   MAYBE   I want a 9-to-5 job with a set schedule.
- Then the military is probably not for you. Military jobs can be orderly and set, with regular hours, but many of them involve working varied hours and an ever-shifting schedule.

YES   NO   MAYBE   I am a hard worker.
- If you are willing to work hard, then military life may be a good fit for you. Your superiors will want to see you giving your all and the service personnel you work with want to be working with someone who can be there for them to help carry the load.

YES   NO   MAYBE   I want to push myself and see what I can accomplish.
- A stint of service in the military is a good personal challenge. During your initial recruit training, what your instructors will

want is for you to give your best effort, especially when you think you can't. Later on in military service, your superiors and your fellow service personnel will want you to be eager to try new things, to learn, and to grow in your chosen field.

YES   NO   MAYBE   I like physical exercise and activity.
- The military requires that its service members be physically fit in order for them to perform their jobs to the best of their ability. Each branch of the service has its own requirements for physical fitness standards, so you will need to consider whether or not you are able to meet or able to train to meet those standards.

YES   NO   MAYBE   I like being outdoors and/or don't mind roughing it.
- While not all military jobs are outdoors, at least during recruit training you will be hiking, camping, learning to navigate outdoor terrain, participating in warfare simulations, etc. If you are sent to war — which is a possibility for everyone who enlists in the military — then you will be faced with living in a variety of terrains, in tents and in other rough conditions. Even those personnel who live on ships or in barracks often live in close quarters with others and don't have many of the luxuries civilians may be used to.

YES   NO   MAYBE   I always do things my way and don't like taking orders from anyone.
- A big part of military life is taking orders, even if those orders seem to make no sense or go against what you may want to do. While the military does train its service members to think ethically and morally and to make judgments for themselves, it also expects people to follow orders and to work with others.

YES   NO   MAYBE   I want to be a leader or a manager.
- Military service is an excellent way to gain leadership experience. The military trains all its service personnel to take on leadership roles, even as early as boot camp. You have to be willing

to start at the bottom, though. Don't assume that you will lead right away. You have to learn how and you have to earn the right to lead.

YES   NO   MAYBE   I work and play well with others.
- Teamwork is a major part of military life. Not only will you be working closely with others in your unit, you will also be living in close quarters — sometimes very close. The military needs people who can handle being around others and working in groups.

YES   NO   MAYBE   I like meeting new people and I can be open to diverse beliefs and opinions.
- Much of military life is meeting new people, whether it is other servicemen and women or people in other countries and from other cultures. Flexibility and openness are important qualities in a service member. The military does not tolerate discrimination and service men and women are expected to be able to be tolerant of the people — both military and civilian — with whom they have to work.

YES   NO   MAYBE   I like to travel.
- You will travel if you join the military, but remember that you won't always get to choose where you will travel to. The military will try to station you in locations where you want to go, but the military's needs always come first.
- If you join the reserves or the National Guard (meaning you will be serving part-time, rather than on active duty which is full-time), then you will be assigned to a reserve unit in your area. This does not mean, however, that you won't travel. Reservists and National Guard members still travel for training or when they are called to war or to assist in relief operations.

YES   NO   MAYBE   I am a conscientious objector. I refuse to fight or participate in any war because of my religious, personal, moral, or ethical beliefs.
- Then you SHOULD NOT join the military. If you try to enlist,

the recruiter will ask you if you are a conscientious objector. If you say yes, then you will ineligible for enlistment. If you lie, then you could face severe penalties later on if you object to being sent to war. The military is a fighting institution. It trains its members to fight, to wage war, and to kill. If any of these seem like they are something you cannot do with a clear conscience, then you should seek out other service options.

YES NO MAYBE   I am okay with some wars, but only if I agree with the government's reasons for waging them.
  • The military exists to carry out government policy. Service personnel are expected to obey their superiors all the way up to the President of the United States, who is the Commander in Chief of the armed forces. Whether or not service members agree with those orders is immaterial. They still have to obey. While in the military you will retain your rights as a United States citizen and can use your vote to try to change government policy, but you will still be expected to fight in the wars waged by the United States until such time as that policy changes.

YES NO   I have dependents.
  • Dependents are any people that you have to take care of: your current spouse; any of your children or stepchildren who live with you or who you support, who are under 18 and unmarried; and any other family members who need you for more than half of their support. The branches of military limit the number of dependents that you can have because they require you to be able to adequately support them financially. Each branch has its own regulations about how many dependents you can have and whether or not having dependents will require you to get a waiver in order to enlist. Your recruiter can tell you more about the policies of his or her branch.

YES NO   I am married.
  • You can serve in the military while married, but you and your spouse should both know that military service can put a strain

on your marriage. You may be away for long periods of time and face stresses that your spouse may not understand. You'll both have to work hard to make your marriage a success.

- If your spouse is already in the military, then you'll need to work with your recruiter and your superior officers to help you arrange to be assigned to duty stations near each other. You should also know that the military has strict policies on fraternization between officers and enlisted personnel, so if one of you is an officer and one is enlisted, this could cause problems during your time of service.

YES   NO   I am a single parent.
- The military will NOT allow you to enlist if you are a single parent with sole custody of one or more children. In order to enlist, you will have to give up custody of your child or children and then often wait several months to a year before being eligible to enlist. If you have joint custody of your child or children, then you will have to fully turn over custody to the other parent during the time in which you are in basic training. Additionally the other custodial parent will have to sign a statement agreeing to that arrangement before you are eligible to enlist.
- Those service members who become single parents while in the military find that single-parenting can often be incompatible with military service. The military requires that service personnel place their jobs before their families. They must be ready to deploy at a moment's notice and must have a local person who will sign a written agreement to take charge of their children with no prior notice. Any violation of a "Family Care Plan" will result in an immediate discharge.

YES   NO   MAYBE   I am not married and I don't have kids, but I want to have a family someday.
- You can have a family and serve in the military. Many military service men and women are married and have children. Most

military bases have childcare facilities, schools, playgrounds, and family housing. There are no longer any regulations preventing women from being pregnant while on active or reserve duty and there are even special pregnancy uniforms. And the tight-knit military community means a built-in support system for your family.

- However, raising a family while serving in the military has its own special challenges. You will likely be away from your family for extended periods of time, missing birthdays, anniversaries, and holidays. Your family will have to move often, usually every three to five years, which means your children will have to change schools and your spouse will need a career where he or she can change jobs often. Military pay, especially enlisted pay and especially for lower ranking enlisted personnel, is not high and it can be tough to make ends meet. And military work puts you at risk for stress, injury, illness, and death, so you will have to make sure that your family is prepared for any eventuality.

YES   NO   I am female.
- Today's military could not operate without its female soldiers, sailors, Airmen, Guardians, and Marines. Women serve in all five branches as both officers and enlisted. With the exception of some adjustments for physical qualifications, women are held to the same standards as men when enlisting in the services. That said, though, there are some things that women who are interested in serving should consider.
- First of all, women in the Air Force, Army, Marine Corps, and Navy are not eligible for all jobs. Combat jobs are off-limits to female service members and women are not allowed to serve in the Special Forces, such as the SEALs. (The Coast Guard, however, has no gender qualifications on any of its career fields.) The military's restrictions do not mean that women do not see combat, though. Military women are still sent to war

zones such as Iraq and Afghanistan and their duties there, as well as the fluid nature of modern warfare, often mean that they see as much combat as their male comrades.

- Second, all potential enlistees need to consider any children they currently have and whether or not they are likely to have children in the future. Women — and men — are allowed to serve in the military while also being parents, but there are many challenges that come with those dual roles. Read the information above about dependents, single parents, and family life in the military.

- Finally, enlistees should know that rape and sexual assault, of both male and female personnel, is a problem in the military. In April 2011, fifteen female veterans and two male veterans brought a lawsuit against the Department of Defense, charging that military commanders did not do enough to prevent sexual assault, to support victims, and to prosecute offenders. According to the Service Women's Action Network, over 3000 military sexual assaults were reported in 2010, though the Pentagon estimates that 70–80 percent of military sexual assaults are unreported. The military has policies about sexual harassment and offenders who are found guilty of rape and assault are dealt with, but many victims say that they are reluctant to bring charges against their attacker or attackers for fear that they will not be believed or that it will adversely affect their careers. The Pentagon is looking into the situation, but at this time it remains a serious issue.

YES   NO   MAYBE   I am homosexual or bisexual.
- In December 2010, President Barack Obama signed a bill into law which overturned "Don't Ask, Don't Tell," the policy which allowed homosexuals to serve in the military only if they did not tell anyone their sexual orientation or participate in homosexual activities (i.e., sex or gay marriage). Though there was much back and forth in court about overturning the policy, it was finally

repealed officially on September 20, 2011. As of that date, men and women serving in the military can no longer be discharged for admitting that they are homosexual or bisexual and potential enlistees are no longer considered ineligible if they are gay. (Transgender persons were excluded from the repeal and transgender persons are not eligible to enlist if they have had a sex change operation.) Service personnel who were discharged under "Don't Ask, Don't Tell" will be allowed to reenlist if they desire.

- Even before the repeal of "Don't Ask, Don't Tell," homosexuals were serving in the military. Estimates say that over 70,000 homosexual men and women are serving in the military as of May 2010 and over a million veterans are gay, lesbian, or bisexual. The repeal is expected to bring in roughly 37,000 new homosexual and bisexual enlistees.

- But even with the repeal of "Don't Ask, Don't Tell," there will still be years of work to do in order to insure that gay service personnel are openly integrated into military life. The first men and women serving openly will likely face harassment, tension, stress, and more, just as the first minorities and the first women did when they integrated into the military, though the military branches are working to insure that troops are trained in the policy that sexual orientation has nothing to do with the military's mission. If you are homosexual or bisexual, you are allowed to enlist and serve, but you will probably have to work even harder to prove yourself during your time of service. At this time the Pentagon is not planning on adding sexual orientation to its equal opportunity policy, so you will probably not have a legal way to fight discrimination and harassment which is based on your orientation.

- Additionally, the Department of Defense (DoD) is restricted by the 1996 Defense of Marriage Act, which limits marriage to that of one man and one woman, so partners of gay service members will not be eligible for certain spousal benefits, such as on base housing or medical coverage. And if even if you are legally married in a state that allows gay marriage, the federal government does not acknowledge your marriage for purposes such as filing taxes or receiving death benefits, so the military cannot recognize your marriage either. However, the Pentagon has ruled that military chaplains are allowed, if they so choose, to perform wedding services for homosexual couples in states where gay marriage is legal. There are likely to be more changes as policies are enacted that address the issues of gay service members.

YES   NO   I am not a United States citizen.

- You can only join the military if you are a United States citizen or if you are a legal permanent resident who has a green card and is living in the United States. The military will not help you immigrate and cannot help your family immigrate after you join. If you have lived in a country that is considered hostile to the United States, then you will have to get a waiver in order to be able to enlist. Additionally, job opportunities for non-citizens are more limited as you will not be eligible for the security clearances needed for some jobs. Once non-citizens have enlisted, however, there are accelerated programs that will help them become citizens.

YES   NO   I am currently having financial or legal problems.

- The military is not a way for you to escape your financial or legal obligations. You will not be allowed to enlist until you have cleared up any financial or legal issues, such as bad credit or scheduled court appearances. Some financial or legal problems could also affect your choice of military jobs, since they could hinder your ability to get a security clearance.

YES   NO   I have a criminal background or have had scrapes with the law in the past.

- You will need to talk with a recruiter about whether or not your past crimes will keep you from being eligible for military service. Criminal waivers are available in some cases, but the requirements vary depending upon the crime. All past brushes with the law will come to light during either the enlistment process or during a security clearance check, so you must not lie or omit information when talking to your recruiter.

YES   NO   I have a physical disability or serious health issue.
• Depending upon what that disability or illness is you may be ineligible for military service. There is a very long list of disabilities and illnesses that will make you ineligible. Recruiters can give you the complete and up-to-date list, as well as tell you if you might qualify for a medical waiver which will allow you to serve despite your medical history.

YES   NO   I am a drug user or have used drugs in the past.
• The military takes drug use very seriously. All service personnel are regularly tested for drug use. If you are thinking about enlisting and are currently using drugs, now is the time to get help and stop. You will not be able to continue using drugs while you are in the service. Even if all you use is tobacco, you will not have access to it during recruit training, so stopping now will make training easier for you.
• If you have used drugs in the past, even if you only experimented a single time, you will need to be honest about your usage when you talk with a recruiter. He or she can let you know if your drug use makes you ineligible for service or if you will need to apply for a medical or criminal waiver in order to enlist. This also goes for legal drugs which were prescribed for you by your doctor (such as Ritalin or antidepressants).

These are some of the things you should consider about your personality, your goals, and your past and present life. It is important to carefully consider all factors before making the decision to join the military. Think about your goals and whether or not a military career is compatible with them. If you want to learn a trade, does the military have jobs you can learn and then apply to a civilian career? Are you eligible for those jobs? What are the limitations on money you'll receive for education? How long will you have to enlist for? Consider all of the negatives and all of the positives of military service and decide if the negatives outweigh the positives for you. Now is the time to think clearly, rationally, and logically. Do your research and consider all options carefully.

Things to Consider
for Parents of
Potential Enlistees

If your son or daughter is considering joining the military, you will probably feel a mix of emotions. You may be proud that he or she is contemplating enlistment, especially if by doing so he or she is continuing a family tradition of military service. But you may also be worried. You may wonder if he or she will be tricked by a crafty recruiter. You may be concerned that your son or daughter may not be able to handle the rigors of basic training. You might fear for his or her life in facing the very real possibility of going to war or fighting. You may want him or her to do something different in life: go to college, get a civilian job, serve in another way. All of these feelings are normal and natural.

The most important thing to remember is that ultimately this is your child's decision. He or she must make the choice that is right for him or her. The military does not want enlistees who were coerced into joining and they don't want enlistees who haven't fully examined their reasons for enlisting. You and your child need to sit down together and discuss all of the options available to him or her. Calmly state your concerns and thoughts, but be sure that your child has enough time to say his or her piece. You need to know what he or she is thinking in order to help him or her make a decision. Here are some possible discussion questions:

- Why are you interested in joining the military?
- What other options are available to you? Can you go to school,

A mom and dad show off pictures of their children who serve in four different branches of the military (Official U.S. Army Photograph by Kari Hawkins, USAG Redstone).

get a job, accept an apprenticeship, do mission work or service work for another agency, etc.?

- What opportunities does the military offer that you cannot get in college, in a private sector job, or in another service organization?
- What pros and cons do you see with military service? What will you gain and what will you have to give up with military service?
  - Go over Chapter 1: Things to Consider with your child to help answer these questions.
- Are you interested in being active duty or in joining the reserves?
  - Either way, he or she will still be gone for basic training and any follow on training. But after that training is over,

reservists return home and serve with a unit close to where they live, assuming there is a reserve unit near them.

- Are you thinking of doing just one tour of duty in the military or are you leaning towards making it a lifelong career?
  - Even one tour of duty is about an eight-year commitment, accounting for both active duty time and time spent in the inactive reserves. More information can be found in Chapter 1.
- Which branch or branches of the military are you interested in? Why do they appeal to you? What do they offer that the other branches do not?
  - Ideally potential enlistees will research all branches of the military before ever speaking to a recruiter, so that they will have an idea which branch or branches might be best suited to their interests and abilities. This book is specifically about the Air Force, but Chapter 5 has basic information about each branch and the other books in the series address the other branches.
- What job or jobs would you like to do in the military? Why is the military the best place to learn and practice that job or those jobs? Are there civilian opportunities to train and work in that field or those fields?
- Do you know anything about life in the military? What housing is available? What services are offered both on base and off? What hours will you work?
  - Military life varies widely depending on if a service member is on base or off, on a ship or not, active duty or reservist, junior enlisted or senior, what job he or she is doing, etc. If you and your family have the time, take a tour of military bases from all branches. Approach the tour as you would a college tour — look over the facilities, talk to people who are living and working there, ask any questions you have. The public affairs personnel on base can help you schedule a tour.

- What benefits — health, medical, financial, educational — does the military offer? What are the limitations attached to these benefits?
- Are you ready to deploy for months at a time if you are assigned to do so? Do you feel capable of dealing with the realities of war? Will you be able to fight and kill if told to do so?
- Have you spoken with any military personnel?
  - Help your child arrange to speak both with personnel serving right now and with retired personnel. Just remember that those who have retired will not have the most up-to-date information on benefits, jobs, life in the military, etc. But they will be able to tell your child how their service changed them for both good and ill.
- What are the enlistment requirements for each branch of the military? Do you meet those basic requirements?
  - Chapter 9 has the basic requirements for the Air Force.
- Do you feel academically ready to take the Armed Services Vocational Aptitude Battery (ASVAB) test? How can I help you prepare?
  - There is more information on the ASVAB in Chapter 13.
- Do you feel that you are in good enough physical shape for military training and service? Are you prepared to improve your physical fitness level so that you will be ready for basic training?
- Are you mentally ready to give up a lot of your personal freedom during your time in basic training and, to a lesser degree, while you are serving in the military?
- How will serving in the military affect your personal life? Is your boyfriend/girlfriend/husband/wife prepared for and supportive of you enlisting?
  - If your child is married, he or she should have his or her spouse look over Chapter 3: Things to Consider for Spouses.

- *If your child has children*: How will you support your children while you are in the military? Is your spouse prepared to be a part-time single parent? *If your child is a single parent*: What are the military's regulations on enlisting as a single parent? What family care plan will you put in place while you are training and serving?
    - Many branches of the military will not allow single parents to enlist. Most require them to give up custody of their children before they are allowed to join. While serving, parents must have a family care plan in place so that their children do not affect their ability to do their military job, which includes being able to be deployed at short notice.
- If you are unable to join the military for any reason, what would you do instead?
- Can I come with you when you meet with recruiters?
    - This will give you the opportunity to ask any questions or voice any concerns you might have. Remember, though, that your child's meetings with recruiters *must* be led by your child. He or she should do most of the talking and most of the responding to the recruiters' queries. You are only there in an advisory and supportive capacity. More information on meeting with recruiters can be found in Chapter 10.
    - NOTE: if your child is 17, then you will have to come with him or her to recruiter meetings and you will have to give your permission before he or she can enlist.

Your child may not have all the answers to these questions at first. The questions are designed to help him or her spot areas where he or she needs to do more research. The best thing you can do is to help him or her find out more about all aspects of military service. Look at both the pros and cons of enlisting. For some people the military is a rewarding lifelong career. For others it is a time when they are paid to learn a trade, while also earning money for their education and while giving back to their country. And some other people discover that military service is not for them. Maybe they have physical issues which preclude service or maybe they decide that their skills, interests, and goals do not mesh with military life. No matter what your child decides, even taking the time to consider military service will teach him or her a lot about who he or she is inside and what his or her goals are for the future.

Things to Consider
for Spouses of
Potential Enlistees

There are a lot of reasons why your husband or wife might be considering joining the military. Perhaps he or she has finally decided to follow a childhood dream of enlisting. Maybe he or she feels a call to service that can no longer be denied. If the job market in your area is bad or if your spouse does not have the appropriate training, education, or skills for the available jobs, then the military might seem like a good option which will allow him or her to support your family. But whatever your spouse's reasons for enlisting, you both need to sit down and talk carefully about what joining the military will mean for your family. Look over the questions for potential enlistees in Chapter 1. The questions will give you an idea of some of the things you and your spouse need to think about when he or she considers enlistment. Here are some other possible discussion questions:

- What opportunities does the military offer our family that we cannot get by you going to college, getting a private sector job, or joining another service organization?
- What pros and cons do you see with military service? What will we as a family gain and what will we have to give up if you enlist in the military?
- Are you interested in being active duty or in joining the reserves?
  - Either way, he or she will still be gone for basic training and any follow on training. But after that training is over,

reservists will return home and serve with a unit close to where they live, assuming there is a reserve unit near them.

- Are you thinking of doing just one tour of duty in the military or are you leaning towards making it a lifelong career?
  - Know that even one tour of duty is about an eight-year commitment, accounting for both active duty time and time spent in the inactive reserves. More information can be found in Chapter 1.
- Which branch or branches of the military are you interested in? Why do they appeal to you? What do they offer that the other branches do not?
  - Ideally potential enlistees will research all branches of the military before ever speaking to a recruiter, so that they will have an idea which branch or branches might be best suited to their interests and abilities. This book is specifically about the Air Force, but Chapter 5 has basic information about each branch and the other books in the series address the other branches.
- What job or jobs would you like to do in the military? Why is the military the best place to learn and practice that job or those jobs? Are there civilian opportunities to be trained and work in that field or those fields?
- What are the enlistment requirements for each branch of the military? Do you meet those basic requirements?
  - Chapter 9 has the basic requirements for the Air Force.
- Do you feel academically ready to take the Armed Services Vocational Aptitude Battery (ASVAB) test? How can I help you prepare?
  - There is more information on the ASVAB in Chapter 13.
- Do you feel that you are in good enough physical shape for military training and service? Are you prepared to improve your physical fitness level so that you will be ready for basic training?

- *If you and your spouse have a child or children:* How will we support our child or children while you are in the military? What will it mean for me to be a part-time single parent while you are training or deployed? What family care plan will we need to put in place while you are training and serving?
- How will our family be taken care of in the event that you are injured or killed while training or deployed?
- What support services exist on base to help military spouses? Will I be left alone for long periods of time while you are gone? How will we keep our marriage strong while you are away?
- What is life in the military like? What housing is available? What services are offered both on base and off? What hours will you work?
  - Military life varies widely depending on if a service member is on base or off, on a ship or not, active duty or reservist, junior enlisted or senior, what job he or she is doing, etc. If you and your family have the time, take a tour of military

Military marriages can be challenging, but there are many rewards as well (Official U.S. Marine Corps photograph by Lance Cpl. Daniel Boothe).

bases from all branches — look over the facilities, talk to people who are living and working there, ask any questions you have. The public affairs personnel on base can help you schedule a tour.

- What benefits — health, medical, financial, educational — does the military offer? What are the limitations attached to these benefits? Do they just cover the service member or do they cover his or her family as well?
  - ○ See Chapter 4: Military Benefits for more information.
  - ○ If you and your spouse/partner are a same-sex couple, you should know that at this time, the military does not offer many benefits to same-sex spouses/partners of military personnel.

These questions are a starting point for you and your spouse to be talking over the possibility of military service. They should help you both learn what areas you need to research further. As your spouse continues to look into the possibility of military service, help him or her. Go to the recruiters' offices with your spouse. (More information on visiting recruiters can be found in Chapter 10.) Help him or her study for the ASVAB and get in shape physically. Whether or not your spouse decides that military service is right for him or her, the journey into the enlistment process offers you the opportunity to learn more about each other and your goals and desires for the future.

Military Benefits

While military men and women give up a lot during their time in the service, they also receive benefits to help them out. Those benefits range from basic pay you receive for doing your job, to allowances for living expenses, to extras like educational benefits. The list of benefits is extensive and varies slightly by branch of service, years of service, job, and rank. You will never get rich working for the military, but the benefits you receive can, when used wisely, help you save money, get an education, and prepare for retirement and/or a civilian career. Your recruiter will have the most up-to-date information on benefits and during your time of service your commanding officers will keep you apprised of what benefits are available to you. There are several resources about military benefits listed in the "For More Information" section as well.

The major categories of military benefits afforded to service men and women are: pay, allowances, and incentives; vacation or leave time; housing and meal benefits; medical coverage; educational benefits; and more.

Pay, Allowances, and Incentives

Basic military pay is the same for all branches of the service, but varies by rank and years of service. An E-1 (the junior-most enlisted rank; an Airman Basic in the Air Force) with less than four months of active duty will make $1357.60 per month as of 2011, but as soon as he or she has over four months of active duty service, then pay will be

$1467.60 per month. Enlisted service men and women who make it all the way to the top of the enlisted ranks (E-9, either a Chief Master Sergeant or a First Sergeant in the Air Force) make between $4600 and $5100 per month at this time. Military personnel are paid on the 1st and 15th of each month.

Military pay tables are available here: *http://www.dfas.mil/dfas/militarymembers/payentitlements/militarypaytables.html*. Each year Congress decides whether or not to raise military pay. The latest military pay charts will be located at *http://www.dfas.mil* under the heading "Military Pay."

In addition to the basic pay, military service members receive allowances. Allowances help cover the cost of housing, uniforms, etc. Housing allowance is for military service members who decide to and are able to live off base. It is designed to help cover the cost of renting or buying a home. If you are stationed in an expensive part of the country or world, then you may qualify for a cost-of-living allowance in addition to the housing allowance. There is also a basic allowance for subsistence which helps cover the cost of food purchased off base. Your clothing allowance helps defray the cost of buying and maintaining your uniforms. After you are issued your initial uniform during basic training, you are given an allowance to help you replace parts of the uniform that have worn out or need updating. This allowance varies depending upon how long you have served in the military. There is also an allowance to help you cover the cost of military moves and an allowance you receive when you are assigned away from your family for a long period of time, usually longer than 30 days. Generally most allowances are not taxable, which means you do not owe the government money for them each year as you do with your pay.

Incentives are the broad range of special pay which some military personnel earn. Incentives may be given based on job, such as working on a submarine or working as a parachute jumper. There is incentive pay for military personnel on flying status and for those assigned on a ship at sea. You can earn incentive pay if you are a diver, if you are proficient in and work with a foreign language, if you are assigned to a foreign country, or if you are stationed away from your dependents for over 30 days and they cannot accompany you. Incentive pay is given for hazardous duty and for service in a combat zone. Additionally, if a military service member serves in a combat zone, then his or her pay received during that time may be exempt from Federal taxes.

Vacation or Leave Time

Military personnel do get time off and they earn vacation time — called "leave" — at a rate of 2½ days per month for a total of 30 days a year, but unlike in civilian jobs, when you are on vacation weekends are counted as part of your leave. However, you do not get to take your vacation whenever you would like. Your time off has to be approved by your supervisor and he or she can deny your request if the military decides they need you to keep working.

Housing Benefits

Most military bases have some form of housing available, but who can live there and whether or not there is room for everyone varies depending upon the size of the base, the location of the base, and other factors. Generally speaking, lower-rank (junior) enlisted personnel who are single must live on base in the barracks. These range from shared rooms with shared baths (much like a dorm room at a college) to small, apartment-like singles where you and another service member share living quarters, but have separate bedrooms and bathrooms. Living in the barracks not only means sharing, it also means you are subject to inspections (both announced and unannounced). If you are assigned to a ship for any reason, your living quarters will be much more basic. Ship's berths are generally communal, as are the bathrooms, and they are small, so be prepared to share.

Air Force housing for junior enlisted personnel looks a lot like college dorm rooms (Official U.S. Air Force photograph by Airman Anthony Jennings).

Junior enlisted personnel are sometimes allowed live off base, but they will not receive a housing or food allowance, so it can be hard to afford it on their pay. As you rise up the enlisted ranks (generally around E-5 in the Air Force), you become eligible to live off base using a housing allowance to help you afford a place of your own.

Married service members can live on base in apartments, duplexes, or separate houses, depending upon what is available on base, what rank you are, and how big your family is. Families can also use their housing allowance to live off base. If you are married to another military member, things are a little trickier, especially if you are in different branches of the service. The military tries to station you together as best it can, but that "best" is usually considered to be at duty stations within 100 miles of each other. And even with the overturn of the "Don't Ask, Don't Tell" policy, gay service members and their partners/spouses are not eligible for married, on base housing.

Meal Benefits

When you live on base in the barracks or if you are assigned to a ship, then you will generally eat in the dining hall. You will receive a basic allowance for food, but most of that will go directly to the dining hall to pay for the meals you are supposed to receive. Personnel living off base or those in houses on base provide their own meals, though they also receive the subsistence allowance to help pay for food.

Medical Coverage

The military, like most employers, offers healthcare benefits to their personnel. Active duty personnel are completely covered for both medical and dental. Servicemen and women can also make sure their immediate family is covered as well, through the military's healthcare plan called Tricare. (Gay service members' partners/spouses are not eligible for coverage. Their biological or adopted children may be eligible, but stepchildren will not be.) Tricare has several different types of coverage. In some of those plans, immediate family members of active duty personnel are completely covered without any extra costs, but with some limitations, while other plans have a yearly deductible. Reserve military personnel are covered during the time they are on active duty, and they can purchase coverage for their family during those times, but otherwise they are not covered. Military retirees no longer get free medical care for life, as they were promised in the past, but they can still belong to Tricare. Your recruiter will have the most up-to-date information on healthcare costs or more information on Tricare can be found at *http://www.tricare.mil*.

Educational Benefits

Many people join the military because of the education benefits. In addition to the job training all military personnel receive, they also have access to programs which can help them earn a college degree, either while serving or afterwards. Through distance education programs, many military personnel can work towards a degree during their off-duty hours, though you should be aware that earning a degree this way takes longer than going to school full-time and in the military it can sometimes be hard to find off-duty time for classwork, depending on what your job is. Bases and ships often offer classes to their personnel, providing the space for professors and students to work. All of the military branches also offer tuition assistance which will cover the cost of classes and fees, though there are limitations on how much they will reimburse you per semester hour (generally around $250) and a cap on yearly reimbursements (generally $4,500).

The most well-known education benefit is probably the GI Bill. There are several variants of the GI Bill, but all new military enlistees are automatically enrolled in what is called the Post-9/11 GI Bill. This new version of the bill adds to and adapts the benefits offered, but still with the goal of helping military service members pay for college. You will usually use your benefits after you leave or retire from the military, though you can also use your benefits while on active duty or in the reserves. The Department of Veterans Affairs, better known as the Veterans Administration (VA), pays your GI Bill benefits directly to your college or university and also offers a stipend of up to $1000 per year to help you cover the cost of books. Veterans and reservists also qualify for a monthly housing stipend as long as they are attending school full-time and not using a distance education program. One new benefit with the Post-9/11 GI Bill is the ability for personnel who have served in the military for at least ten years to transfer their GI Bill benefits to their spouses or children. GI Bill benefits are limited to 36 months and must be used within 15 years of leaving active duty service. You must have been discharged from the service honorably in order to receive GI Bill benefits.

You do not have to be planning to go to a two- or four-year college to use your GI Bill benefits. The benefits also cover you if you are planning on taking a correspondence course, receiving flight training, participating in a non-college degree program (such as beauty school or truck driver training), accepting an apprenticeship, or doing on-the-job training (as in police academy training or plumbing). Your benefits can help you pay for training and can offer you supplemental income as you work your way to a new career.

The VA also has a program to support the children and spouses of military personnel who were killed in action or permanently disabled. It is called Survivors and Dependents Assistance. You can receive this benefit even if you are military yourself and it can be combined with the GI Bill benefits to give you up to 45 months of educational support. It cannot, however, be used for correspondence course training.

Additionally every branch except the Air Force has a type of college fund. These funds, sometimes referred to as a "GI Bill Kicker," are in addition to the amount that you will receive through the GI Bill. The amounts you hear mentioned in ads for the military (i.e. "$40,000 for college") are the amount you will receive through the GI Bill added to the amount you will receive from the college fund. You cannot receive the college fund without getting the GI Bill, but with the college funds it is the military branches, not the Veterans Administration, that decide who is eligible.

Other Benefits

There are a wide variety of other benefits open to military personnel. Bases often have "commissaries" (grocery stores) and "exchanges" (department stores) for personnel and their families to shop. These facilities are on base, do not charge sales tax, and usually have slightly lower prices than comparable stores in town, which can save you and your family some money and time when you are picking up essentials, though the selection can be limited depending upon the size of your base. Morale, Welfare, and Recreation services are available for personnel and their families and they include recreation centers (which offer everything from discount tickets to shows and attractions to classes to family fun programs), gymnasiums for keeping fit, child development centers for families where both parents work full-time, libraries, and more. And if you serve active duty for twenty years, then you can retire with most military benefits and military retirement pay.

The Branches of
the Military

If you decide that a military career might be a good fit for you, you'll then need to decide which branch of the service you might be interested in. You should to talk to recruiters from all branches of the service, even if you think you know which branch you want to join. They can give you an idea of what their branch has to offer, tell you about how their branch is structured and what the enlistment requirements and expectations are, and help you to find out if their branch is good fit for you in terms of its culture and its job offerings.

Which Branch to Join?

This volume focuses specifically on the Air Force, but before going into detail about the Air Force, we'll look at all of the branches of the military in general, each separately covered in the companion books. There are five branches of the military: the Army, the Navy, the Air Force, the Marine Corps, and the Coast Guard, from largest to smallest.

ARMY

The United States Army is the oldest of the United States' military branches, founded in June 1775, and also the largest. Its main job is to fight on land using ground troops, tanks, helicopters, artillery, etc. As of September 2010 there were 561,378 people serving on active duty in the Army (not counting cadets at the United States Military Academy):

94,128 officers and 467,248 enlisted. Of those numbers, 15,070 of the officers were female and 60,377 of the enlist personnel were female, about 13 percent of the Army's force. The Army also has two reserve units: the Army Reserve, which is run by the federal government, and the Army National Guard. Each state maintains its own National Guard units, rather than them being controlled by the national government. In 2009, there were 645,394 personnel total in the Army Reserve and the Army National Guard.

Army Emblem (United States Army).

NAVY

The United States Navy was also founded in the summer of 1775, though it was disbanded after the Revolutionary War and not officially reinstated until 1794. The Navy is the United States' sea-based branch of the military. Its mission is to fight battles at sea using ships and submarines. The Navy

Navy Seal (United States Navy).

works closely with the United States Marine Corps to accomplish that mission. The Navy also uses its large aircraft carriers to launch air attacks and can launch land attacks using long-range missiles. 323,745 personnel — 52,364 officers and 271,381 enlisted — were serving on active duty in the Navy in April 2011 (not counted midshipmen at the United States Naval Academy), with 8,184 female officers and 43,438 female enlisted personnel or almost 16 percent of the Navy. The Navy does have a Reserve component and 109,271 personnel were serving in the Navy Reserve in 2009.

AIR FORCE

The United States Air Force is the youngest branch of the military, formed after World War II by the National Security Act of 1947. It is the aviation branch of the military and uses its resources to defend the United States in the air and in space. It has a wide variety of aircraft for fighting, transport, bombing, rescue, etc. The Air Force is also responsible for all military satellites. In September 2010, 329,638 service men and women were active duty in the Air Force (not counting cadets at the United States Air Force Academy), with 66,201 officers and 263,437 enlisted. Women made up 19 percent of those numbers, with 12,363 women serving as officers and 50,946 women serving as enlisted. The Air Force has a Reserve component and there are Air National

Air Force Seal (United States Air Force).

Guard units in each state. In 2009 there were 220,364 personnel serving in both.

MARINE CORPS

The United States Marine Corps started during the Revolutionary War, but wasn't officially established as a separate branch until 1798. The Marine Corps is closely connected with the United States Navy. The Marine Corps' mission of amphibious warfare — launching land attacks from sea — is a good complement to the Navy's sea-based mission. The Marines also train forces in ground combat and use aircraft and helicopters to attack. They use the Navy for medical support and some administrative support. The Marines are a small service, with about

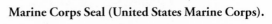

Marine Corps Seal (United States Marine Corps).

201,623 people serving on active duty in September 2010. At that time there were 21,307 officers and 181,134 enlisted, about 7.5 percent of which were female (3,054 officers and 12,203 enlisted). There is a Marine Corps Reserve, comprised of 95,199 personnel in 2009.

COAST GUARD

The Coast Guard, which began as the Revenue Cutter Service in 1790, plays a unique role in the United States military. They handle boating safety, law enforcement, search and rescue, and other tasks related to maritime security. Unlike the other branches of the military, which operate under the Department of Defense, the Coast Guard is part of the Department of Homeland Security, though during times of war control of the Coast Guard can be transferred to the Navy, if so ordered by the President. In September 2010 the Coast Guard had 42,358 personnel on active duty: 8,508 officers and 32,837 enlisted, not counting cadets at the United States Coast Guard Academy. 5,552, or 13 percent, of these active duty personnel were women. There is a Coast Guard Reserve (with 9,399 personnel in 2009) and a volunteer, unpaid Coast Guard Auxiliary.

Even if you are positive that you only want to serve in the Air Force, it is to your benefit for you to learn about each of the branches of the military. The different branches do not operate completely independently and if you decide to enlist in the Air Force it is very likely that you will find yourself working with service members from other branches.

Coast Guard Seal (United States Coast Guard).

Next, in Part Two, we'll talk more specifically about the Air Force, looking at its history as well as what career opportunities are available for you in the Air Force.

Two

General Information About the Air Force

6

The History
of the Air Force

The Air Force is the newest branch of the military, officially founded in 1947, but it can trace its origins back to before the Civil War, as new aviation innovations began to develop military applications.

Early History

You probably already know that brothers Orville and Wilbur Wright were the first people to successfully fly an engine-powered airplane when they took off at Kitty Hawk, North Carolina, on December 17, 1903. But militaries have been using aeronautical methods to aid in battle since well before the Civil War. Homing pigeons have been used for communications purposes as far back as the Middle Ages. Other methods of communication such as smoke signals also relied on the air. Balloons, however, were to be the first aerial war transports.

In 1783, French brothers Joseph-Michel and Jacques-Étienne Montgolfier, along with two friends, became the first men to successfully lift off in a basket hung from a balloon. Balloons began to be brought to the United States and in 1840, Army Colonel John H. Sherburne proposed using them as aids for locating the Seminole Indians during the Seminole War. The Army was also offered the chance for balloons to use in aerial bombing runs during the Mexican War in 1846, but it did not take advantage of the opportunity.

During the Civil War, several balloonists offered their services to the Union cause, with sporadic success. While some balloon operators never managed to get their balloons to cooperate in order to perform reconnaissance, others were useful to Union troops. John LaMountain made sketches of artillery and enemy positions while aloft. Thaddeus S.C. Lowe was able to direct artillery fire and send telegraphic messages while aloft. Lowe was even captured as a Union spy and sent to prison. Balloon reconnaissance was also used during the Spanish-American War in 1898 as part of the newly reorganized Signal Corps (the communications branch of the Army), but afterward the Army did not do much with balloons — or the dirigibles which followed — and they were soon both supplanted by the newest technology — the airplane.

After their initial flight in 1903, the Wright brothers focused on further developing their new airplane. They received offers from the British government in 1904 to buy their plane, but refused, wanting the American people to benefit from it first. They offered the plane to the Army starting in 1905, but could not convince the War Department

This exact replica of the Wright brothers' first plane shows how delicate early aircraft were (Official U.S. Air Force photograph).

that they had developed a practical flying machine. When President Theodore Roosevelt began showing interest in the airplane, things slowly began to change. The Signal Corps established an Aeronautical Division in 1907 and by 1909 had purchased its first airplanes from the Wright brothers and from the Aerial Experiment Association, a group founded by Alexander Graham Bell. Research continued on how to adapt the airplane for war, but Congress did not approve funds for aviation until 1911. European nations, on the other hand, had been heavily investing in flight. By the time the First World War broke out, the United States was not prepared to fight in the air.

World War I (1914 to 1918)

New legislation was passed in 1914 to establish the Signal Corps' Aviation Section, which would have sixty officers and 260 enlisted men. The First Aero Squadron, which had originally been established in 1913, was reorganized and began to prepare for combat duty. The Squadron flew a mission against outlaw Pancho Villa at the Mexican border in 1916, but that mission was not a success. The planes could not handle high mountain ranges, blizzards, windstorms, and other environmental factors. The aviation program was not ready for combat. Congress finally began to appropriate funds to the Signal Corps to use for aeronautical development, though by that time there was barely any staff in the Aviation Section to handle that kind of money and no research facility to facilitate aircraft improvements.

By 1917, when the United States joined the United Kingdom, France, Russia, and the other Allies in fighting against Germany and Austria-Hungary, the First Aero Squadron was still the only fully equipped air unit in the Army, and it only had about 250 training planes and no fighters. Additionally, only American pilots who had flown with British or French units had any combat experience. The Army had to lean heavily on the European forces for training, materials, aviation research, and expertise with aviation combat. In 1918 the Air Service of the United States Army (originally founded by General John J. Pershing earlier in the year) was combined with the Signal Corps' Aviation Section, the Bureau of Aircraft Production, and the Division of Military Aeronautics. It only served in nine months of the war, but during its time of service it downed 756 enemy craft. Otherwise, many American aviators fighting in World War I were part of British or French squadrons.

World War I was a time of great advancement in aviation fighting. Pilots went from simply scouting out enemy positions to actually engaging enemy planes. After Dutch engineer Anthony H.G. Fokker perfected a machine gun which could fire between the blades of a plane's propellers, air battles called "dogfights"—where each plane shoots at the

Captain Rickenbacker was a race car driver before becoming a World War I ace fighter pilot (Official U.S. Air Force photograph).

other and tries to knock it out of the sky — became part of war. One American pilot, Captain Edward Rickenbacker, was a World War I "ace" (a pilot who had shot down five or more enemy pilots) when it came to dogfights. He shot down 22 enemy aircraft and four balloons, earning himself a Medal of Honor.

Planes themselves changed drastically over the course of the war. At the beginning of World War I, most airplanes were biplanes. They had two wings: one above the open cockpit and one below. They were made of wood and canvas and could only fly about 75 miles per hour. But by 1918, planes were made of more durable materials and could fly as fast as 120 miles per hour. New mechanical devices were created to drop bombs automatically, rather than the pilots having to drop bombs by hand out of a bag they carried in the cockpit. Other types of aviation equipment were also used during World War I, such as reconnaissance balloons and airships used for bombing, but it was planes that made headlines. The United States benefited from the experience of war, moving from fourteenth place in the aviation world to fifth in just two years.

World War II (1939–1945)

After the First World War, the air forces began to ask the government for their own branch of the military. The most outspoken proponents were Generals Benjamin Foulois and Billy Mitchell. General Mitchell had commanded American, British, French, and Italian air forces during a September 1918 battle which ended in an Allied victory. He thought that air forces needed to be separate from ground forces, but he was so vocal in criticizing the government's decision to keep the aviation program as part of the Army that he was court-martialed for insubordination. (In 1946, after time had proven that General Mitchell had been correct, he was awarded a Medal of Honor.)

The 1920s was a time of record setting aerial feats. The first aerial refueling occurred and pilots strove to break speed and distance records. During the time between the world wars, the Air Service — which became the Air Corps in 1926 — began to develop new types of planes, including the first all-metal bomber in 1931. In 1931 the government divided aviation into two types: land-based, in control of the Army, and naval, in control of the Navy. The Army's land-based aviation was given the go-ahead to begin developing the use of long-range bombers to destroy an enemy's important industrial sites, such as ammunition factories, roads where supplies are transported, etc. This led to the test of the first B-17 bomber in 1935. Other innovations such as the closed cockpit, bomb rack, and retractable gear began to appear on aircraft.

When Adolf Hitler's army attacked Czechoslovakia in 1938, President Franklin Roosevelt began to take steps to boost aircraft production in anticipation of war. On December 7, 1941, Japanese planes attacked the United States Naval Base at Pearl Harbor, Hawaii, bringing the U.S. into World War II. That same year, all of the aviation elements of the Army had been combined into the U.S. Army Air Forces under the command of General Henry H. "Hap" Arnold, a famed pilot who had learned to fly from the Wright brothers themselves. The Army Air Forces used large bomber craft to fly missions in Europe to destroy German factories and other sites. Fighter planes began to accompany those bombers to protect them, leading to fierce air battles between Allied and Axis air forces. In the Pacific, the Army Air Forces flew nighttime bombing missions over Japan, using firebombs on 66 Japanese cities. Those raids were leading up to the Army Air Forces' most devastating new attack — the atomic bombings of Hiroshima and Nagasaki in 1945.

Women and minorities were important parts of the fighting forces during World War II. The Women's Air Force Service Pilots (WASP) program was established to use white female pilots to transport servicemen and supplies between United States bases. The Women's Auxiliary Ferrying Squadron (WAFS) ferried planes around the world, freeing male pilots to fly fighting and bombing missions. The two groups were later combined into one. One thousand and seventy four women graduated from WASP training and, along with 28 WAFS, flew almost every type of plane in the United States Army Air Forces. They were even used to fly the B-26 Marauder, nicknamed the "Widowmaker," a plane that male pilots thought was too dangerous to fly until women showed them it could be done. Thirty-eight WASPs and trainees were killed during their service but because WASPs were considered to be civilians, they received no pension or benefits after the war. Colonel Jackie Cochran was in charge of the WASP program. She was the first woman to break the sound barrier (in 1953) and during her career she held the most speed, altitude, and distance records of any pilot, male or female.

Some African American men were allowed to join what was called "Tuskegee Airmen," launched in 1941 by President Franklin Roosevelt. The Army Air Corps' school in Tuskegee, Alabama, trained black pilots, meteorologists, flight surgeons, mechanics, and more. Captain Benjamin O. Davis, Jr., who later became the first African-American general of

The Tuskegee Airmen were an important part of the war effort (Official U.S. Air Force photograph).

the Air Force, was the commander of the Tuskegee Airmen. The Airmen flew over 15,000 sorties and almost 1,600 missions, including over 200 bomber escort missions over Europe between June 1944 and April 1945, during which time they did not lose a single bomber to the enemy. Still considered during the war to be second class citizens, the Tuskegee Airmen were finally recognized and awarded a Congressional Gold Medal in 2007 to thank them for their service.

Post–World War II, the Korean War (1950–1953), and the Vietnam War (1957–1973)

The Army Air Forces' strong performance during World War II and its role as the first military service to drop an atomic bomb allowed it to make the case for independence once again, even though rapid demobilization after the war had left the Army Air Forces with hardly any operational squadrons. After much contentious debate between the Army, the Navy, the Marine Corps, and the Army Air Corps about the role of airpower in future wars, the National Security Act of 1947 created the United States Air Force and made it an equal partner with the United States Army and the United States Navy. The Berlin Airlift of 1948 was the new Air Force's first big job. American, British, and French forces flew food into Germany to help supply the people of West Berlin who were trapped behind a Soviet Union blockade.

The late 1940s proved to be momentous in other ways as well. In 1947, Captain Chuck Yeager broke the sound barrier in his X-1 rocket powered aircraft. The Women's Armed Services Integration Act of 1948 allowed women permanent status in the regular and reserve forces, though with restrictions on numbers and promotion levels which continued until 1967. Executive Order 9981 was also drafted in 1948, ending racial segregation in the military, though the Air Force had been integrating units since 1947.

In the early 1950s, United States forces joined South Korea in its fight against North Korea, which was being assisted by China. Air Force planes fought close air battles over the Yalu River near the China border in an area nicknamed "MiG Alley" after the Soviet MiG fighter planes. New jet fighters, such as the F-86 Sabre, were used and the Air Force worked closely with Navy and Marine Corps airmen to protect ground fighting forces. By the end of the conflict, the Air Force had downed about 900 enemy aircraft. The conflict ended without a clear victory, but the Air Force kept a number of units stationed in the Pacific to assist with containing the communist threat.

The Vietnam War was a conflict between forces in South Vietnam and those in North Vietnam, which were supported by the Soviet Union and China, as well as the Viet Cong rebels in South Vietnam. The United States joined to support the South Vietnam forces and between 1961 and 1973 the Air Force dropped more bombs in Southeast Asia than were dropped by both sides during World War II. Laser-guided bombs, which rarely missed a target, were introduced during the Vietnam conflict. Helicopters were also more widely used in Vietnam than in any previous war. Despite U.S. and other forces' efforts, the Vietnam conflict ultimately ended in victory for the North Vietnam troops.

The reserve components of the Air Force began to rise during the 1940s. The U.S. Air Force Reserve was established on April 14, 1948, and reservists first saw combat during the Korean War when every flying wing of the reserve, 25 all told, was mobilized along with almost 119,000 individual reservists. In the 1950s the Air Force spent time tweaking its reserve program, fixing problems which had emerged during wartime. Reservists participated in the Vietnam War in the late 1960s along with the Air National Guard. The Guard was established as a separate reserve unit in 1947, but had been working in aviation since before World War I. Several states had small flying programs and in 1915 New York founded the First Aero Company of New York which participated in the border fight with Mexico in 1916. National Guardsmen were volunteers in World War I and Guard personnel were added to the Army Air Forces during World War II. In the Korean War, 80 percent of the Guard was called to service, but were found to be unprepared for combat, forcing the Air Force to rework its reserve program, leading to a stronger, better equipped Guard during the 1960s and 70s.

The 1950s and 1960s saw a lot of social upheaval and scientific changes in the Air Force. The Air Force Academy was established in 1954, though the first African American did not graduate until 1963 and women would not be admitted until 1976. As nuclear bombs continued to develop into new and much more powerful weapons, the Air Force built planes that had jet engines and nuclear capabilities. The Air Force was also responsible for developing intercontinental ballistic missiles (ICBMs), which could be launched from land. The Soviet Union was also developing ICBMs at the same time, leading to the Cuban Missile Crisis, a stand-off between the United States and the Soviet

Technology has always been important to the Air Force. During the Cuban Missile Crisis, it helped U.S. forces keep track of what the Soviets were doing in Cuba (Official U.S. Air Force photograph).

Union that began when the Soviets began installing ICBMs in Cuba in 1962. The Soviet Union finally backed down and removed the missiles, but tensions were high for several weeks. The space program was begun in earnest, drawing many of its early astronauts from the ranks of the military. Space became a new frontier for the Air Force. Many of the first astronauts were Air Force officers and by 1962 the Air Force has a system of satellites which circled the Earth, gathering information about the weather and about other countries. The Air Force's Space Command was established in 1983, laying the ground work for the Department of Defense's unified U.S. Space Command to be founded in 1984.

1970s through 1990s

During the late 1970s through the 1990s, the Air Force and the other military branches found themselves in a period of change. The draft was ended in 1973 and the military became an all-volunteer service. In 1971, Jeanne M. Holm became the first woman in the Air Force to be promoted to General and in 1974 laws were changed to allow women to continue serving in the military even while raising families. Congress repealed laws banning women from flying combat aircraft in 1992. With the fall of the Berlin Wall and the end of the Cold War, the Strategic Air Command was shut down in the early 1990s.

The Air Force fought in or assisted during wars in the 1980s and 1990s. Operation El Dorado Canyon was a joint operation between the Air Force and the Navy striking at targets in Libya in reaction to terrorist attacks directed by dictator Muammar al-Qadhafi. The Air Force also helped with the overthrow of Panama's dictator General Manuel Noriega in 1989. When Iraq invaded its neighbor Kuwait in August 1990, the Air Force began a massive airlift of over 577,000 tons of supplies and 498,000 military passengers in preparation for the beginning of the first Persian Gulf War in January 1991. During the war, the Air Force only lost 14 aircraft during more than 37,000 combat flights and they dropped hundreds of laser-guided bombs. In 1995, the Air Force attacked Bosnian Serb rebels as part of a North Atlantic Treaty Organization (NATO) mission to assist Bosnian Muslims as part of the war in Bosnia-Herzegovina (1992–1995). Serbian forces attacked Albanians in the province of Kosovo in 1999 and the Air Force helped provide NATO air strikes to end the attacks.

Recent History

Following the terrorist attacks of September 11, 2001, Air Force forces helped with rescue efforts at the disaster sites in New York City, Washington, DC, and Pennsylvania. Air Force planes patrolled the skies above the United States, on the lookout for more attacks. On October 7, 2001, the United States military began a campaign in Afghanistan against al-Qaida and Taliban forces, leading to the overthrow of the

In Afghanistan, an Airman enters a home to search for explosives (Official U.S. Air Force photograph by SrA Grovert Fuentes-Contreras).

Taliban government. The Air Force struck airfields, command centers, training camps, and more, preventing Taliban forces from getting fighters off the ground. Since combat operations began, the Air Force has flown more than 85,000 sorties, including airlift missions moving over 500,000 passengers and 500,000 tons of cargo. The Air Force continues to support ground operations in Afghanistan. Before the beginning of the 2003 Persian Gulf War, the Air Force carried supplies to staging areas around Iraq, mostly in Kuwait. Airstrikes began on March 20, 2003, and the Air Force used precision-guided bombs to attack Iraqi targets and ground troops for over four straight days, virtually wiping out Iraq's air forces. Iraqi dictator Saddam Hussein and his ruling Baath party fell in 2003 and the United States wrapped up combat operations in Iraq. The Air Force was a major part of that successful mission.

The Air Force is now focused on modernization, to make sure that it continues to have the strongest, most efficient systems in place to face down future threats to the United States and overcome them.

7

Career Opportunities
in the Air Force

Obviously one of the most important things you should consider when you begin comparing the different branches of the military is what jobs will be available to you in each branch. The recruiters you visit will help you learn about the career fields available in each branch, but you will be better off if you do some research before you enlist. That way you will know which job fields appeal to you and be able to make the decision that is right for your future.

What if you already know exactly what military career field you want to be in? You should still look at everything that is available. Many factors can prevent you from entering a particular field — the military may have too many people already doing that job, your test scores may show that the job is not a good fit for you, that job may not be open when you are ready to begin training, or the job may have restrictions which you cannot meet. If you have already looked at all the jobs available in each branch, then you can decide if you want to try for another job or if another branch may offer you a better chance to achieve your dream.

What if you don't know what military career field you might be interested in? Reading over all of the options available in each branch might give you some ideas, but your recruiter can help as well. The Armed Services Vocational Aptitude Battery (ASVAB) test that you take during enlistment will show you and your recruiter what career fields you are best suited for. (We'll talk more about the ASVAB testing process in Part Three.) Also, each branch of the military will have jobs that they are eager to fill. Your recruiter can tell you what those are and if you are qualified. So if you truly don't care what job you do, then you can allow yourself to be placed in one. But that should be a last resort only undertaken if you truly don't care whether you are a chef or a mechanic or a human resources specialist or something else completely.

The type of job you want to do might depend upon whether you want to work in a hands-on field or if you prefer a field where you are dealing with abstract concepts such as information, numbers, or words. You also want to think about if you prefer primarily working with machines or primarily working with people. Do you want to be in an exciting, ever-changing, possibly dangerous career or do you think you'd rather have a job with more stability? Are you more of a science and math oriented person or more of an arts and letters oriented person? These are all things to keep in mind as you consider the types of jobs the different military branches have to offer.

Your recruiter can tell you which jobs are open to you. At this time, women are not allowed to sign up for jobs designated as combat positions, though the United States government is considering changing that rule. (However, this doesn't mean that women in the military don't see combat. Many female service personnel serve in jobs that still send them into danger and near or even into the frontlines.) Some jobs are not open to enlistees who will be going into the reserves — only active duty personnel may fill those jobs — and reservists are usually limited in jobs depending upon the needs of their assigned unit. Other jobs, such as Special Forces, are not ones you can be guaranteed. If you meet the qualifications for consideration, you will be evaluated during your early training to see if you are a good candidate.

Whatever career field you pick, in whichever branch of the military, you will be working in that career field for at least the next four to eight years, so it is in your best interest to pick something that you think you will enjoy. If you enlist, the military is going to spend a lot of time and money training you, so it wants you to be in a job where you will work hard and excel. In Part Three you will learn about talking with your recruiter about your job possibilities. For now, let's look at what type of jobs are available in the Air Force.

Air Force Enlisted Careers

Many people assume that the only jobs in the Air Force are either piloting a plane or working on some highly technical computer. But actually the available jobs have plenty of variety, so there is something for everyone who is interested in becoming an airman. Air Force jobs can be broken into several broad categories:

- Working with Aircraft
- Working with Weapons
- Working in Construction and Engineering
- Working with Materiel and Non-Aircraft Vehicles
- Working with Computers and Intelligence
- Working with People
- Working in Medical Fields
- Working in Safety and Security
- Working in Public Affairs and the Arts

Let's take a look at each of these broad categories and the types of jobs that fall under each one.

Working with Aircraft

Of course some of the most important jobs in the Air Force are done by those men and women who work on and with the Air Force's fleet of planes, helicopters, and other aircraft. There are opportunities for working as part of a flight crew, for working on the aircraft on the ground, and for a variety of other jobs that are necessary parts of the Air Force's mission.

Working as part of a flight crew can be an exciting and challenging job. You'll be part of a highly trained, hard-working crew who are focused on completing important missions. There are a number of jobs open to enlisted personnel who are interested in on board careers. You might be the person operating the airborne command and control systems or you might be the Aerial Gunner — in charge of operating, maintaining, and inspecting airborne weapons. For planes that refuel in mid-air, an Airman is needed to be in charge of that refueling. Airmen are also needed to operate, evaluate, and manage intelligence, surveillance, and reconnaissance during flight. Others are needed to take charge of cargo and passengers before, during, and after flights.

On the ground, personnel working with aircraft are responsible for keeping the Air Force's airfields running smoothly. Air Traffic Controllers coordinate all takeoffs and landings from an airfield, as well as organizing the planes in the air above the airfield. Meanwhile personnel working in Airfield Management maintain the airfields and also act as first responders during emergencies. Other Airmen are responsible for keeping records of each day's flights. An Aviation Resource Management Apprentice signs aircrew members in and out, making sure that they have met the physical and safety requirements for flight. While that is happening, Airmen working in Air Transportation are in charge of the loading, unloading, and inspection of all cargo.

Planes break down and many people are needed to get them up and running again. Every type of aircraft in the Air Force needs a repairer to specialize in its avionics systems. (Avionics are the electronics of an aircraft.) Other professionals are needed to work on the hydraulic systems, the fuel systems, the metal components, and the bodies of the aircraft. There are Airmen who specialize just in the equipment used by flight crews, making sure it is ready for any contingency.

Working with Weapons

Weapons are an important military resource. When you're working on an aircraft's armament systems — inspecting, loading, maintaining, and repairing the munitions on board each aircraft — you are insuring that the aircrew can complete their assigned mission. Airmen with top security clearances are needed to be responsible for the Air Force's Intercontinental Ballistic Missile (ICBM) systems — the long-range missiles that can carry nuclear weapons. Jobs are available for Airmen who want to learn to repair and maintain these systems or for those who want to work with nuclear weapons. If you would rather learn how to get rid of weapons, then you might be interested in the dangerous

An aerial gunner surveys the skies above Afghanistan (Offical U.S. Air Force photograph by SrA Tyler Placie).

Weapons load handlers make sure aircraft have the ammunition they need (Official U.S. Air Force photograph by Tech. Sgt. Lindsey Maurice).

and challenging job of Explosive Ordnance Disposal. Airmen who work in that field detect and render inoperable all types of unexploded bombs and devices.

WORKING IN CONSTRUCTION AND ENGINEERING

If you have ever longed to be part of a construction crew, then you can still pursue that dream in the Air Force. Airmen work in all aspects of construction, from heating, ventilation, air conditioning, and refrigeration to utilities and from construction with wood, stone, and concrete to working as an electrician. There are Airmen who drive heavy construction machinery and Airmen who are responsible for pest control. Other Airmen learn to install, maintain, and repair the many cables, warning systems, devices, and navigational, meteorological, and radio systems needed on airfields and bases.

A Senior Airman uses heavy equipment during construction of a pipeline (Official U.S. Air Force photograph by Master Sgt. Scott T. Sturkol).

Working in an engineering job means that you are helping to build, repair, and improve all of the Air Force's facilities, aircraft, and resources. Engineering Apprentices do surveys and create drawings to help craft new bases and airfields. Airmen working in labs do research to identify defects in metal equipment or to align, troubleshoot, and calibrate equipment. You might be interested in working in Operations Management, where you will work with civil engineers to coordinate the building of roads, bridges, etc.

WORKING WITH MATERIEL AND NON-AIRCRAFT VEHICLES

Airmen are necessary for keeping the large amount of cargo supplies moving smoothly throughout the Air Force. Personnel working in Materiel Management coordinate the movement of all supplies, in order to get cargo to the airfields to be loaded onto aircraft. Contracting

A materiel management journeyman inspects a gas mask to make sure it is fully operational before it is sent to Airmen in the field (Official U.S. Air Force photograph by Master Sgt. Chance Babin).

Apprentices are Airmen learning the ropes of buying all of the Air Force's supplies and equipment, as well as paying for all services and construction projects. Airmen in Traffic Management are the ones who make sure shipments are ready for transport and those in Logistics Plans make sure that deployments are well-planned and well-organized.

The Air Force doesn't just use planes to travel. Airmen working in Vehicle Operations are the drivers and operators of all of the cars, trucks, and other transport vehicles in the Air Force. All of those vehicles need repair and maintenance just as the aircraft do and there are Airmen who specialize in scheduling and coordinating the maintenance of the motor pool. Other Airmen specialize in repairing the motor pool vehicles when they break down.

Working with Computers and Intelligence

The Air Force's focus on technology means that many Airmen are needed to install, operate, analyze, and repair the Air Force's computer and data systems. You may be working with radio frequencies, sensors,

Transmissions systems radio technicians must operate in all types of weather conditions (Official U.S. Air Force photograph by Senior Airman Natasha E. Stannard).

or even Morse Code to help gather and interpret information. Some Airmen work on computer networks. They may develop software, install hardware, or work on insuring the security of cyber systems. Other Airmen analyze transmissions — voice, noncommunications transmissions, and video images — or even still photos, to collect data important to their mission. Still others are responsible for gathering weather data from radars and satellites.

WORKING WITH PEOPLE

While all of the jobs in the Air Force require that you be willing and able to work well with others, there are some jobs in which people, rather than equipment or vehicles, are your main focus. The Air Force needs people to act as human resources staff, assisting, advising, and keeping track of Airmen and their dependents. Other Airmen are responsible for keeping the financial records of the Air Force. Airmen in the Services jobs are working in a career similar to those in the hospitality industry. They may be in charge of recreation facilities, food services, mortuary affairs (working with deceased Airmen and their dependents), or in laundry/linen facilities.

WORKING IN MEDICAL FIELDS

All of the Air Force's personnel and their dependents will need medical care at some point in time. Many Airmen work in medical careers, some directly working with patients and others working in a laboratory situation. Enlisted Airmen can work as dental hygienists, surgical assistants, pharmacy technicians, x-ray technicians, or assistants to physical therapists, nutritionists, eye doctors, or mental health staff (psychiatrists, psychologists, social workers, and mental health nurses). If you work in a laboratory, you might be a Histopathology Apprentice, preparing slides and specimens for analysis and assisting in autopsies, or you might work in a medical or dental laboratory, doing medical tests or preparing dental appliances for patients. Airmen in Health Services Management keep medical records, while those in Public Health control communicable diseases, make sure facilities are sanitary, and inspect food supplies. There are also opportunities for those who want to learn to repair and maintain biomedical equipment.

Airmen who work in the Air Force's dining facilities are committed to providing healthy, delicious meals (Official U.S. Air Force photograph by Staff Sgt. Chris Willis).

Working in Safety and Security

Emergencies can occur at any time and the Air Force wants to be ready for them. Airmen working in Emergency Management are responsible for making sure that their base is prepared for enemy attacks, war, and natural disasters. Airmen are also trained to be firefighters and Security Forces (military police). Also working in law enforcement are Airmen who are Paralegals, assistants to military lawyers. Other Airmen teach survival skills to their fellow Airmen and to other military personnel and civilians. Command

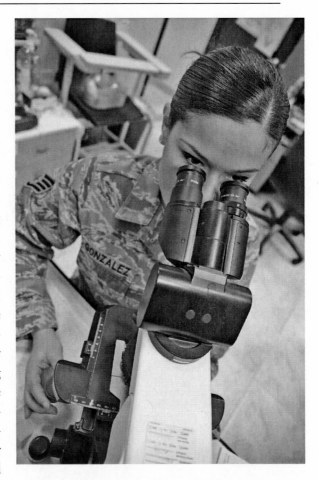

A medical laboratory technician checks a patient's urine sample for disorders (Official U.S. Air Force photograph by Master Sgt. Carlotta Holley).

Post Apprentices work at operations centers to keep Air Force commanders apprised of emergencies, disasters, and other situations. Those working in Aerospace Physiology make sure that aircrew members have the skills to operate at high altitudes and to correctly handle emergencies occurring in-flight.

A firefighter fuels his truck in preparation for assisting with humanitarian relief efforts (Official U.S. Air Force photograph by Airman 1st Class Andrea Salazar).

Band members will often travel as much as Airmen in other jobs. Here an Air Force musician shows off his guitar to Afghan children (Official U.S. Air Force photograph by Senior Airman Sheila deVera).

WORKING IN PUBLIC AFFAIRS
AND THE ARTS

There are also careers in the Air Force for enlisted personnel who are creative and artistic or who like to organize information. Information Management Airmen handle official publications, manage official records, and make sure that the Air Force is communicating effectively. Public Affairs Apprentices assist in the development of informational material to distribute to the public and to news media. Other Airmen work in radio and television broadcasting, helping to produce radio and film programs for the Air Force. Still Photography Apprentices are the photographers of the Air Force and there are many Air Force bands that need talented and experienced musicians.

Now that you've learned more about the Air Force, the next step is to talk to an Air Force recruiter. Even if you are not one hundred percent certain that you want to join the military in general or the Air Force in particular, you should still visit a recruiter. He or she can answer any questions you might have and can give you the information you need to make your decision. In Part Three, you'll learn about the enlistment process, what it entails, and how you can prepare for it.

THREE

The Enlistment Process

What Is the Enlistment Process?

The enlistment process is the steps that take you from civilian to military recruit. It is an important process, filled with decisions that need to be considered soberly and at length. The choices you make during the enlistment process will shape your life for at least the next eight years and should shape the rest of your life, assuming you take full advantage of the training and educational opportunities afforded you during your military service. That means that you need to think carefully about all the options presented to you. You will receive a lot of information and advice from the recruiters you speak to, from your friends and family, and from research you do yourself. It is your job to compile all of that information and advice into a complete picture of what your options are. Until you give the Oath of Enlistment as you are leaving for basic training you are not obligated to anything, so take your time and make the decision that is right for you.

There aren't clearly defined steps that make up the enlistment process, since the experience is different for every recruit and the process varies depending upon which branch of the service you choose to enter. But there is a rough outline that each enlistment process will follow:

- Researching the different branches of the service and getting a general idea of what they are like
- Speaking with recruiters from all branches of the service
- Deciding which branch you are most interested in
- Completing paperwork detailing your past medical, legal, finan-

cial, and academic history to make sure that nothing in your past would prevent you from enlisting

- Taking the Armed Services Vocational Aptitude Battery test (the ASVAB) to see if you are qualified for that branch and to see which jobs you qualify for
- Visiting a Military Entrance Processing Station (MEPS) to get your physical
- Resolving any final physical, moral, or other waivers needed before being accepted into your chosen branch
- Taking the oath to enter the Delayed Entry Program
- Using your time in the Delayed Entry Program to get into physical and mental shape before basic training
- Visiting MEPS to take the Oath of Enlistment and leave for basic training

In this part, we are going to break down the enlistment process into easy to follow sections. First we'll talk about the basic eligibility requirements for entering the Air Force. Next we'll discuss who recruiters are and what you can expect when you visit them. Then we'll cover the basics of the Armed Services Vocational Aptitude Battery test (the ASVAB). We'll move on to talk about Military Entrance Processing Stations and what happens in them. Finally we'll talk about the Delayed Entry Program and how to use it to get yourself in the best possible shape, both mentally and physically, before you leave for basic training.

Eligibility Requirements

Gone are the days when a recruiter could sign up an unwary young man in the morning and have him ship off to basic training in the afternoon. Today's military requires that its enlistees meet a lengthy list of requirements. In order to see if you meet those requirements, your recruiter and the personnel at the Military Entrance Processing Station (MEPS) you visit will look at your mental, physical, and moral qualifications. You will have to fill out an application, submit medical documentation, undergo a physical, and more. This is done so that the military is certain it is selecting the brightest and best young men and women to serve. Even minor physical or moral issues can become major problems on a battlefield and the military wants to catch them before that happens.

Before you even meet with an Air Force recruiter, you can get an idea of whether or not you might be qualified to enlist. The basic eligibility requirements are what a recruiter looks at when he or she meets you for the first time.

Basic Requirements

- Be between the ages of 17 and 27
    - 17-year-olds need their parents' permission to enlist
- Be a United States citizen or a legal permanent resident
    - There are some restrictions on immigrants from countries deemed hostile to the United States
    - Non-citizens will not be eligible for jobs requiring security clearances
- Be a high school graduate

- o Only a very few GED holders are allowed into the Air Force each year
- o Your chances of enlisting with a GED increase if you have 15 or more college credit hours
- Score at least a 36 on the Armed Services Vocational Aptitude Battery (ASVAB) test
  - o Or at least a 65 if you have a GED (more information on ASVAB scores in Chapter 13)
- Be 58–80 inches tall and able to meet the established weight standards for your height. The height/weight standards can be found here: *http://airforce.com/height-weight*.

If you do not meet these basic requirements, then you will more than likely not be able to continue with the Air Force enlistment process. Each branch's enlistment requirements are a little different, so if you do not qualify for one, you can always try to apply for one of the others. But the basic requirements are similar enough that you are better off trying to fix the issues that make you ineligible, such as your weight or your score on the Armed Services Vocational Aptitude Battery (ASVAB) test.

Alternatively, you can see if there is a waiver which would allow you to enlist despite not meeting some of the requirements. But waivers are a lot of work for recruiters and other military personnel, so they only want to do them for potential enlistees who are outstanding in other ways, such as those who speak a needed foreign language or who have extremely high ASVAB scores.

In addition to the basic eligibility requirements, there are some other factors to be considered. These can make you ineligible for Air Force service or might require a waiver in order to allow you to enlist (more on waivers in Chapter 12).

Other Eligibility Factors

- Tattoos: The Air Force does not allow you to enlist if you have tattoos that cover more than 25 percent of a body part, such as an arm or your torso. Tattoos must not be sexually explicit, racist (including rebel flags), discriminatory, or gang related (including praying hands). If your tattoo has foreign symbols or words the Air Force will verify the translation of those symbols or words to make sure your tattoo really says what you think it says.

- Body piercings: Females are allowed one hole in each earlobe. Otherwise body piercings must be removed and the holes healed (in the case of ear plugs and the like) before you are eligible for enlistment.
- Dependents: If you have any dependents (children) under the age of 18, then you will need to get a waiver to enlist in the Air Force. Single parents with sole custody of their children are ineligible to enlist. You may not give up custody of your child(ren) in order to enlist and if you do so, you may not try to regain custody of them after enlistment. Single parents with joint custody must have the approval of the other parent in order to enlist. The other parent must agree to care for the children during basic training.
- Drug and alcohol use: You are ineligible to enlist if you use illegal drugs and/or abuse alcohol. Your recruiter will ask about all previous drug use and you will be given a drug test as part of your enlistment physical and at basic training. You should answer truthfully about all drug use, even casual experimentation. Your recruiter will be able to tell you if your prior drug use makes you ineligible or if a waiver will be required in order for you to enlist.
- Prescription drugs: You are ineligible to enlist if you are dependent upon prescription drugs, including insulin and ADHD medications. The one prescription exception is birth control pills which are used for birth control only, rather than to regulate your cycle. Your recruiter will have more information on which drugs may disqualify you for service and how long you will need to be off of them before being eligible for enlistment.

But *do not* discontinue any legal use of prescription drugs without the consent of your primary physician.

- Medical history: Certain medical conditions will prevent you from enlisting. You will be required to reveal your medical history to the military and you will undergo a physical during your enlistment process. The doctors examining you will determine if any medical conditions are temporary (meaning you can enlist once your condition improves) or are disqualifying (meaning you cannot enlist or that you will need a waiver in order to do so).

- Criminal history: Some criminal convictions will render you ineligible for military service. You must disclose any prior criminal history (even sealed juvenile records) to your recruiter in order to apply to enlist. He or she will be able to tell you whether or not your criminal record makes you ineligible or if you will require a waiver to enlist.

All of these eligibility factors are considered when the Air Force is making the decision on whether or not you are eligible for enlistment. Some factors cannot be waived and will prevent you from enlisting, but these factors can vary between the branches. So if you are still interested in military service, but cannot enter the Air Force, you should still speak with recruiters for the other branches and see if you might be eligible to serve with them.

Improving Your Chance for Eligibility

Before you begin the enlistment process there are some very simple steps you can take to make yourself a more eligible candidate.

- Finish school and further your education:
  - *If you are still in high school, stay there.* Do not drop out and do not waste your time. Study. Do your homework. Make decent grades (aim for at least a C+ average in all of your

classes and you will do fine when you take the ASVAB). Try to take a mix of basic classes (math, science, English, history) and more technical ones or ones related to a field you might be interested in (computers, business, journalism, etc.).

- o *If you have finished high school, take classes at your local community college.* General education classes (math, science, English, history) will not only keep your mind fresh for the ASVAB, but getting them done now will save you time later if you decide to work towards your degree while serving in the military. Take your classes seriously, though, and strive to make decent grades.
- o *If you have dropped out of high school, you MUST get your GED before you can even consider enlisting.* Additionally, it is recommended that you have 15 credit hours of college classes under your belt. This will put you on the same consideration level as a high school graduate.
- Visit your family physician:
  - o *You should get a full physical out of the way before beginning the enlistment process.* Not only will this alert you to any problems which might hold up your enlistment, but your family doctor can advise you whether or not you can stop taking any drugs that have been prescribed for you. He or she can also tell you how to get in shape for enlistment.
- Exercise and eat right:
  - o *According to a 2010 study at Cornell University, almost 12 percent of young men and over 30 percent of young women who are the right age for enlistment are ineligible due to not being able to meet weight standards.* Now is the time to lose weight, eat right, and exercise more. Your doctor is the best guide for this process. Never try to lose weight or begin an exercise program without consulting him or her first. Now is also a good time to stop smoking. It will improve your health and make you a stronger candidate.

- Avoid risky behavior:
  - *Do not drink (if you are underage) or drink excessively, use illegal drugs, break the law (including traffic violations), get tattoos or body piercings, bounce checks or get into financial trouble, have unprotected sex, etc.* All of these behaviors could lead to issues which will hinder your ability to enlist.
- Instead form healthy habits:
  - *Volunteer. Take up a hobby or a new sport. Get a part-time job. Take a class on a subject which interests you. Learn a new language. Stay current on the news.* All of these will keep your mind and body active and healthy, which will ultimately make you a better candidate for military enlistment.

Talking to
Military Recruiters

Recruiters are active duty military personnel who are specially trained to select the young men and women who will join the branches of the service. They are your point of entry into the military, in general, and the Air Force, specifically. To put it simply, it is their job to decide if you are a good fit for the Air Force and if the Air Force is a good fit for you. Their advice can help you make the best decisions for your future. As has been mentioned before, you'll want to make sure that you meet with recruiters from all the branches of the service. An Air Force recruiter can only answer questions accurately about the Air Force and as each branch has something different to offer, it is in your best interest to meet with them all in order to get the most information on your options.

Meeting Your Recruiter

There are several ways in which you might meet an Air Force recruiter. If you take the Armed Services Vocational Aptitude Battery test (ASVAB) in high school, then your scores are usually shared with local recruiters. Assuming your scores are high enough to qualify for enlistment, recruiters will contact you, usually by phone. You may also give your information to the Air Force and request that a recruiter contact you. The easiest way to do this is to go to www.airforce.com and click on "Contact Us" at the top of the page. Calling your local Air Force recruiting station is a good option as well or you may meet a recruiter

Recruiters often go to schools so that they can meet interested young people (Official U.S. Air Force photograph).

at a community event. Recruiters are often out in the community and in schools, looking for likely candidates for military service.

However you meet your recruiter, you want to be sure that you are comfortable with him or her. The recruiter is going to be your entry point into the Air Force and you need to be able to trust that he or she has your best interests in mind. The vast majority of recruiters are loyal, hardworking, honest, professional men and women who want to make sure that they are adding the best of the best to the Air Force. They will tell you the truth and expect it from you in turn. Recruiters are trained in persuasion, much like salesmen, but they are also trained to act as your representative as you navigate the enlistment process. They do not work off of quotas, though they do have goals to meet each year.

But those goals are often easily achieved and recruiters then have the luxury of being picky about the new enlistees they sign up.

However, there are a few recruiters who may not be completely aboveboard. If you ever feel uncomfortable about a recruiter for any reason, then you should stop working with them immediately. Look for another recruiter in the same branch of the service, but in a different office and explain — politely and calmly — why you have concerns about the first recruiter you spoke to. Your concerns will be taken seriously and looked into, especially if you are respectful about how you present them. If you are not comfortable speaking with another recruiter, because of anything that the first recruiter may have said or done, contact Air Force Recruiting Service (contact information is in the back of this book, under "For More Information").

Additionally, if you don't feel that you are completely "clicking" with your recruiter, speak to the other recruiters working in the same office. Personalities vary and you may find a better rapport with another recruiter.

Initial Meeting with a Recruiter

Once you have made contact with an Air Force recruiter, he or she will ask you to come in for an initial interview. This will give you a chance to learn more about what the Air Force has to offer you and for the recruiter to learn more about you, so that he or she can make sure you are qualified to enlist in the Air Force. That initial meeting with your recruiter is a job interview, so you should treat it as such and take it seriously. Here are some important tips:

- Before going into the meeting, do some basic research on the Air Force so that you will know more about its mission, history, careers, etc.
- Make an appointment and keep it. If an emergency comes up and you need to reschedule, call the recruiter immediately.
- Leave early enough so that you will not be late to the meeting.

Don't forget to account for traffic and time to find a parking spot. Some recruiting offices can be tricky to locate, so you might want to get directions online or from the recruiter.

- Dress nicely — dress shirt, slacks, and possibly a tie for young men; a modest dress or a skirt or slacks with a blouse for young women.
- Turn off your cellphone or leave it in the car. Same for MP3 players.
- Shake hands, greet the recruiter by name and rank, and thank him or her for taking the time to meet with you.
- Be an active listener. Listen to everything the recruiter says and be sure to ask for clarification of any details you don't understand. Ask questions and listen carefully to the answers. Don't be afraid to ask "stupid" questions.
- Be open and honest. The military will do background checks on you, so you might as well tell the truth from the beginning.
- Be professional and respectful. You are interviewing the Air Force at the same time that the Air Force is interviewing you. Treat this as you would any job interview. If you've never interviewed before, look for some books on interviewing at the library or for interview tips online.

The recruiter will tell you if there is anything specific he or she needs you to bring with you, but you should always bring your:

- Driver's license
- Social Security card
- Birth certificate
- High school diploma
- College transcript (if applicable)
- Permanent resident alien (green) card (if applicable)

There are other items that are a good idea to bring with you. These will save both you and the recruiter time and will help you make sure you have all the information you need:

- A pen and a pad of paper for taking notes.
- Your parents or legal guardians.
  - They will have questions too and many recruiters prefer that they be a part of the initial interview process. If you do not wish to include them or if you are not in contact with them, then you can bring a mature friend or a trusted adult. They are there to help you remember what is discussed. But know that the recruiter needs to ask personal questions about past drug use, medical issues, and more, so be sure that you are okay with talking openly in front of the person who accompanies you.
  - Note: If you are 17, then your parents must come with you and their approval is required for you to be able to enlist.
- Your spouse.
  - If you are married, your husband or wife should come with you. If you have children, though, they should stay with a baby-sitter so that you can have uninterrupted time to talk with the recruiter.
- Your résumé listing any jobs you've held since you were 16.
  - Also bring the names of your supervisors and the addresses and phone numbers of your past and present jobs.
- Medical information.
  - Bring what you know, but you will need to give the military a complete profile during the enlistment process, so the more information you can gather beforehand, the better.
- Information about any law violations, even minor ones like traffic tickets and even ones where your juvenile record was sealed.
- Names and phone numbers for several personal references, people who can speak to your character and personality.
  - These should not be family members. Make sure they have agreed to speak to any recruiters who call them.
- Goals you would like to accomplish in your life.
  - If the recruiter knows what you want to do, then he or she can help you see how the military might be able to help you meet those goals.

You should also bring any questions you have for the recruiter. These can be anything you want to know about the Air Force, the enlistment process, basic training, military service, etc. Think about these carefully and then type them out on a computer, so that you can easily read them. Again, don't be afraid to ask questions you think are dumb. The recruiter wants to answer all your questions and it's almost a guarantee that he or she has heard every question you could think to ask. Some possible questions:

- Can you explain the enlistment process to me from beginning to end?
- How does the Air Force differ from all other branches of the service?
  - o You should know the basic answer to this from your research, but this will give the recruiter an opportunity to fill in any blanks.
- What do you like about being an Airman? What do you dislike? Why did you become an Airman?
- Can I speak with people whom you have recruited into the Air Force, both recently and in the past, so that I can find out more about their experiences in the Air Force?
  - o Current service members are excellent sources of information. Remember to speak to them as politely and respectfully as you do the recruiter. Ask them about their experiences during the enlistment process, basic training, follow-on schooling, and in their first assignments. Ask them if they are enjoying their work and if they plan on re-enlisting. Ask them what their impressions of your recruiter were.
- For potential enlistees who are female: Are there female Airmen I could speak with about their experiences?
  - o They will be able to tell you what it is like to be a woman in the Air Force. Be sure to talk to both new female Airmen and ones who have served for some time. They will give you different perspectives.
- For potential enlistees who are homosexual or bisexual: Are there gay Airmen I could speak with about their experiences?

- This request will probably be harder for your recruiter to fulfill, since gay service members have not been serving openly before 2011. Ask them about the experience of transitioning from serving under "Don't Ask, Don't Tell," about the experience of serving openly, and about any problems or issues they've face because of their sexual orientation.
- Can I visit an Air Force base or a reserve unit?
  - If you live near a base or a reserve unit this is a great way to see the Air Force in action before you enlist.
- What are the job possibilities available to me in the Air Force? What job did you do before you became a recruiter? Why did you pick that job? What did you enjoy about it? What didn't you like about it?
- How long are enlistment contracts for? How many years will I still obligated to the military after I finish my time in active duty?
  - Even after you finish your active duty commitment, you will still owe the military several years in the inactive reserves, where you can be called back up if needed.
- What rank will I be after basic training? Am I qualified to enter the service at an advanced rank?
  - This usually requires college credit, receiving Eagle Scout or the Girl Scout's Gold Award, several years' participation in JROTC, or a longer enlistment contract.
- How do promotions work in the Air Force? How often will I be promoted?
- Does the Air Force offer opportunities to move from enlisted to officer if I so choose?
- How do I choose my job in the Air Force? Is my career field guaranteed after I finish basic training? Does my chosen job have a comparable civilian job?
- How will I be trained after basic training? What is job training like in the Air Force — mostly classroom settings or more hands on (or does it depend on the job)?

- How am I assigned to my first duty station? How often will I have to move?
- What is the likelihood I will be sent to war or deployed overseas?
  - This varies depending on the branch of the service. The Air Force's mission makes it responsible for protecting the United States from the air and in space. Because today's modern wars require the technical skills that Airmen possess, the likelihood of being sent to help fight is high.
- How often will I travel as part of my job?
- What is basic pay? What supplemental pay and allowances are offered? What will I be required to cover from my paycheck (uniforms, etc.)?
- What education benefits does the Air Force offer? What strings are attached to any education benefits? How does the GI Bill work?
- What are benefits for spouses and families? What is life like on base? What type of housing will be assigned to my family?
- What enlistment bonuses are available? What are the requirements and the restrictions?
  - The Air Force does offer enlistment bonuses, which are tied to jobs it considers critical and/or undermanned. However, enlistment bonuses often come with strings attached: longer contracts, limited job selection, higher ASVAB scores, etc. You should never enlist solely to get a bonus. Your recruiter will have the most up-to-date information on bonuses.
- How do I make sure that what I sign up for (jobs, bonuses, benefits, rank, etc.) is what I actually get? What information is on my enlistment contract?
- What retirement plan is guaranteed for career Airmen? How many years do I need to put in? Will I still have health care when I retire?
- What is Air Force basic training like?

- This is covered in Part Four but your recruiter will have the most up-to-date information.
- Am I in good enough shape for basic training? If not, what would I need to do to improve?
- Can I contact my family during basic training?
- What happens if I get hurt or sick while I'm at basic training? What happens if I am unable to complete basic training for any reason?
- What programs do you offer during the Delayed Entry Program to help me prepare for basic training and military service?
- Can I come to the meetings and training sessions you have with new enlistees who are in the Delayed Entry Program?
  - This will give you a chance to see how the Air Force help new enlistees prepare. You will also be able to get a feel for the culture of the Air Force.
- Can I change my mind about joining the Air Force while I am in the Delayed Entry Program?
  - As long as you have not taken the final Oath of Enlistment — which you take just before leaving for basic training — you are able to change your mind. Once you take the Oath, however, you are obligated to follow through on your contract.
- If I leave the Air Force after my initial enlistment period, what services are available to help me transition back into civilian life? What happens to me if I have to leave before my enlistment contract is up?

These questions, asked during your initial meeting with your recruiter, will allow you to learn more about the Air Force, but the Air Force will also want to know more about you. You will fill out a nonbinding application, which will give the recruiter the information he or she needs to see if you are tentatively qualified to enlist. You may also, at the recruiter's suggestion, take a mini version of the ASVAB in the recruiter's office. It will give you your basic score (which will tell you if you may be eligible for enlistment) and will let you know approximately how well you'll do on the full ASVAB test. (More on the ASVAB test in Chapter 13.) But you should *not* schedule any other testing at this time. The full ASVAB and your physical can wait until you are certain that you want to join the military and until you know which branch you want to enter.

The most important thing to remember about your initial meeting (and any follow-up meetings) is to listen actively. That means pay close attention to what the recruiter is saying and ask questions to further clarify. Do not let your mind wander. Do not get caught up in the excitement of dreaming of a star-spangled military career. There is time for that later. Now is when you need to be objective. Listen closely, ask questions for more information or to clarify, and take careful notes on what you hear. This is very important as you will need those notes later to compare the different military branches.

You should listen carefully during your meetings with a recruiter (Official U.S. Air Force photograph by Staff Sgt. Jennifer Lindsey).

Second Meeting with a Recruiter

Take the information you learn during the initial meeting and think carefully about it for several days. Discuss the meeting with your parents or with the person who accompanied you. Consider whether the recruiter answered all of the questions you asked. Write down any new questions that occur to you. Compare what you've learned about the Air Force with what you learned during your meetings with the other branches of the service. This will help you see which branch will be the best fit for your goals and your personality.

The recruiter should, as you are leaving the initial meeting, schedule a follow-up meeting with you. If he or she does not, then request one. It should take place a few weeks after your initial meeting. The second meeting will be the time for you ask any final questions before you decide if you are going to choose the Air Force, if you are going to choose another branch of the service, or if you are going to choose not to enlist at this time or at all. The second meeting doesn't have to be as long. Take the time to ask any follow-up questions and then thank the recruiter for his or her time. Tell him or her that you will get back to them in a few days to let them know your decision. By this point, you should have met with recruiters from all branches so that you can make a fully informed decision.

Making Your Decision

If you decide that you would rather join a different branch, politely tell your recruiter that you have decided that branch will be a better fit for you. He or she might ask why you decided that the Air Force was not for you. You can tell them if you like, remembering to be respectful. He or she may also try to convince you to give the Air Force another look, but should ultimately wish you well. Do not allow any friendly (or non-friendly) feelings for a particular recruiter to change your mind. Your decision should be based solely on the research you have done and comparison between the branches to see which one best matches your goals and your personality.

If after your research, you ultimately decide that military service is not for you, thank your recruiter for taking the time to speak with you. Be polite, but firm, and tell him or her that you are not interested at this time. Tell him or her why you are putting off military service at this time. Your recruiter might have a suggestion for how you can serve anyway, if you so desire. For example, if you prefer to go to college full-time, then your recruiter might suggest you consider the reserves or apply for an ROTC scholarship. If you simply cannot or do not want to join at this time, but you think you might be interested at a later date, then you can tell him or her that you will get back in touch. However, if you think you will not ever want to join the military, say so. Recruiters want to hear the truth from you.

If you decide you do want to enlist in the military and the Air Force is the branch for you, then your recruiter will start the process of making sure you are fully qualified to enlist in the Air Force. You are not guaranteed entry into the Air Force or any other branch of the service. Your recruiter may agree that you are provisionally qualified for enlistment, but there are a number of physical, mental, and moral factors that have to be looked at before you can be completely cleared for enlistment.

The Qualification Process

After you decide that you definitely want to enlist in the Air Force, the next step is to fill out an enlistment application. This is a form which will follow you throughout the enlistment process all the way to basic training and will be the basis for getting approval to enlist and for your enlistment contract. That means everything on this form needs to be accurate, so read it slowly and carefully, asking questions about any sections you do not understand. Your recruiter will make sure that the information is filled out properly.

The most important thing to remember about the enlistment process is DO NOT LIE. Lying in order to enlist in the military is a felony and when — not if — the military discovers the lie, you will be prosecuted and discharged. You *must* answer all questions truthfully and you *must* provide information to the best of your ability. You will fill out forms to disclose every detail of your medical, legal, financial, and educational history. You must tell the truth about:

- Any past drug use (prescription or illegal)
- Any medical problems that were diagnosed and treated by a doctor (as opposed to ones you only suspect you might have, such as undiagnosed asthma or a "trick" knee)
- Any troubles with the law (even minor ones such as traffic violations and even ones where your juvenile record was sealed or expunged)
- Any pending legal actions (such as being a witness in a court trial or currently going through a divorce)
- Any financial issues (such as bankruptcy or bounced checks)

Air Force recruiters goes over the enlistment application with an interested applicant (Official U.S. Air Force photograph by Master Sgt. Thomas Deering).

Not only should you never lie, but your recruiter should never ask you to lie or to omit information. If your recruiter asks you to change any information, if he or she tells you to leave something off of a form, or if he or she tells you to lie about any aspect of your history, then stop the enlistment process *immediately*. End all contact with that recruiter and report him or her to the Air Force Recruiting Service. (That contact information is located in the "For More Information" section in the back of the book.)

Depending on your history, you might have some difficulty gathering all the required information. If you've lived and worked and gone to school in one town your whole life, you'll have an easier time finding the needed paperwork than if you've moved around your entire life. But your recruiter can help you hunt down missing information, and by talking to family members, school teachers and counselors, your doctor, and other professionals in your life you should be able to find everything. The more data you collect before you first meet with a recruiter, the less time will be spent searching for it after you make the decision to enlist.

Once you have filled out all of the required forms, your recruiter and other military personnel will go over them. They will be able to tell if you are qualified enough to continue in the enlistment process. There are some issues which will stop the process instantly. For example, if medical personnel at a local Military Entrance Processing Station (MEPS — the location where you go for your physical and to take the ASVAB) look at your medical questionnaire and determine that you have a serious medical issue which will not allow you to pass the required physical, then you will not be allowed to continue in the enlistment process. Unfortunately, there is almost no way to get around such a problem and you will not be allowed to join the military.

Some issues will render you ineligible, but might be able to be resolved with a waiver. Whether or not something can be waived is up to the main recruiting office, not your individual recruiter, though he or she can tell you if something definitely cannot be waived. Waivers take a lot of paperwork and you are more likely to get one if you have only minor issues needing to be waived, rather than if you have major problems. For example, if you smoked pot once three years ago and have never done any other drugs at any time, plus you have an application which otherwise qualifies you, then you are more likely to be approved for a waiver than if you have used drugs more regularly and have other problems which would delay the qualification process.

In addition to revealing any negatives from your past, you should also remember to detail any positives. The Air Force does allow you to enlist at a higher rank (E-2 or even E-3, rather than E-1) if you have done several successful years of ROTC or if you completed a high school JROTC program successfully; if you are an Eagle Scout in the Boy Scouts or have received the Girl Scout's Gold Award; or if you have completed twenty semester hours (for E-2) or forty-five semester hours (for E-3) of college classes. Your education background can help your military liaison at MEPS as he or she is helping you pick your job, especially if you already have advanced training or a degree in a specialized area, such as mechanics, computers, music, etc. And volunteer work and other such initiatives show that you are a hard-working person who would be an excellent addition to the Air Force.

After your recruiter has made sure your enlistment application is completely filled out, that all of the information is accurate, and that you do not need any waivers in order to continue the enlistment process (or that you have received the waivers needed to continue), then you are ready to visit MEPS for your physical and to take the ASVAB.

Visiting the Military Entrance Processing Station (MEPS)

Military Entrance Processing Stations (MEPS) are Department of Defense facilities which exist to help evaluate and process potential military enlistees. They are located in almost every state, as well as Puerto Rico, and both civilians and members from every branch of the military work there. Thousands of applicants a year go through MEPS — getting physicals, taking the Armed Services Vocational Aptitude Battery (ASVAB) test, selecting military jobs, signing enlistment contracts, taking the Oath of Enlistment, and leaving for basic training.

Most enlistees will visit MEPS at least twice. The first time is for processing and evaluation of your physical and mental eligibility for enlistment. The second time is for final swearing in and departure for basic training. But everyone's circumstances vary and your MEPS experience will be shaped by any snags in your qualifications, by how far you live from a MEPS facility, by your type of enlistment (active duty or reserve), or by the branch in which you are enlisting. This chapter will give you the basic information on what to expect at MEPS so that you will be better prepared for your visit or visits.

Staying Overnight

Your recruiter will schedule your visit to MEPS after you have completed the initial qualification process discussed in Chapter 11.

Because he or she wants to be sure that you are on time and ready for your day or days at MEPS, generally you will be required to stay overnight the evening before at a hotel near your MEPS location. Your recruiter will make arrangements for your travel and lodging. Your food and hotel stay will be covered by the government, but it is important that you continue to behave professionally and maturely. At this time you are still being considered as an applicant for military service and any mistakes in judgment are likely to end your enlistment process immediately.

While you are at the hotel, you should:

- *Be respectful of your fellow applicants.* You will be sharing a room with at least one other applicant and you will not have a say in who your roommate is. Be polite and courteous and remember that much of military life is learning to work with those who are assigned to your team.
- *Be respectful of the other patrons of the hotel.* Do not make too much noise talking, watching TV, or playing music.
- *Be respectful of the military and the government.* They are covering the cost of your hotel room, but you will be liable for any additional charges. Do not make long distance calls or charge movies or internet service to the room. Remember to listen carefully to the instructions of the military liaison that is in charge of the applicants staying at the hotel. He or she is responsible for making sure that you know the rules and that you get to MEPS on time.
- *Get to sleep early.* Days at MEPS begin early and your wakeup call at the hotel will be as early as 4:30am. Don't stay up too late or you will not be ready for the long day ahead of you. If you're worried that you won't be able to sleep in the unfamiliar environment, you might try sleeping with earplugs in. They can help block strange noises which might keep you awake.
- *Relax.* This is especially important if you are going to be taking the ASVAB the next day. Don't spend time cramming for the

test. It's more important that you rest up so that your brain is fresh for the test. (More on taking the ASVAB in Chapter 13.)

The military liaison will tell you the wakeup time. You will not have a lot of time to get ready (good practice for when you're in basic training!), so you might want to shower the night before. You should wear comfortable, neat clothing. You don't have to dress up, but you should look professional. A good suggestion is "business casual"—slacks and a nice shirt with closed toe shoes and socks. Do not wear hats, clothes with profane or obscene language and images, or jewelry/body piercings. (You'll just have to take any jewelry off for the medical examination anyway, so you might as well leave it at home where it will be safe.) You must wear underwear, including a bra for women.

Arriving at MEPS

After you are ready and you have eaten breakfast, you will be transported to MEPS for processing. It is important that you remember to bring everything with you that you will need, as you will not be able to return to the hotel to retrieve forgotten items.

Items to bring with you to MEPS include:

- Social Security card
- Birth certificate
- Driver's license
- Permanent resident alien (green) card, if applicable
- Eyeglasses and/or contacts and your prescription, if applicable
- Your medical history (your recruiter will help you get this together)
- Pen and paper, in case you wish to take notes on anything
- A book or magazine to read (you are NOT allowed to bring electronic devices, including cellphones, handheld games, MP3 players, etc.)
- Any other paperwork that your recruiter tells you to take

When you get to MEPS, you will pass through the metal detector and then you will begin the processing. Much of the visit to MEPS follows the old military adage of "hurry up and wait," so remember to be patient and to listen carefully to what MEPS personnel tell you to do.

The first visit to MEPS will usually include the following steps:

- Taking the ASVAB (unless you have already taken it within the past two years)
- Getting a complete physical, including blood work
- Talking to a representative from your branch about career opportunities
- Signing your enlistment contract
- Taking the Oath of Enlistment to enter the Delayed Entry Program (DEP); more on DEP in Chapter 14)

If you have not yet taken the ASVAB, or if you need to retake it for some reason, then that will usually be the first thing you do at MEPS.

It is important to pay attention to instructions while you are at Military Entrance Processing Station (Official U.S. Army photograph by D. Myles Cullen).

Some enlistees will take the ASVAB on the afternoon of the first day and then return to MEPS the next day for the rest of their processing. Others will take the ASVAB first thing in the morning and then finish their processing that day. That leads to a very long, very stressful day, though, so it is best to avoid that if you can. Your recruiter will be able to tell you what your options are for taking the ASVAB during your MEPS visit. Chapter 13 tells all about the ASVAB test and the various ways in which it can be taken.

Medical Examination

Whether or not you have taken the ASVAB previously, you will definitely be getting your physical done while at MEPS. MEPS medical personnel will have already looked over your medical files, before you even arrive. The medical information you provided on your enlistment application was sent to MEPS for an initial pre-screening. This pre-screening allows MEPS personnel to rule out applicants who have obvious, major problems. It also gives them a chance to let your recruiter know if more information is needed about a medical issue from your past. That allows the recruiter to work with you to gather that information, so you can bring it with you when you visit MEPS. Then MEPS medical personnel will consider both that information and the information they gather via your medical exam to decide if you are qualified for enlistment, if you need a waiver in order to qualify, or if you are not qualified.

The doctors and nurses at MEPS are not tied to any particular branch of the military and they see potential enlistees from all five branches. Their job is to make sure that you are medically fit for military service. They are not trying to weed anyone out for personal reasons or because they are vindictive and they are not being overly picky about problems that may seem minor to you. They must consider the effect that a seemingly minor medical condition could have on a military unit during battle. They do not want to jeopardize the lives of military personnel by sending someone into battle who will not be able to hold up under fire. They also do not want to put you at risk by sending you for training with a medical issue which will lead you getting hurt or killed.

In order to get a full picture of your medical history and your current physical condition, the staff at MEPS give you a complete physical. This includes:

- Height and weight measurements — including a body-fat measurement if you exceed the weight requirements for your intended service
- Hearing and vision tests
- Range of movement tests — the doctors and nurses will make you stand in a line, wearing only your underwear (males and females are tested separately) and perform a series of movements designed to show problems with your bones, joints, ligaments, tendons, and muscles
- Blood work — for drugs and alcohol, HIV, pregnancy, and general health
- Urinalysis — for drugs and general health
- Medical interview — MEPS personnel will go over the information you provided on your enlistment application and ask you further questions about your medical history. As with the enlistment application, DO NOT LIE
- Specialized tests — if the doctors or nurses decide they are necessary in order to follow up on a suspected issue or problem

There are a lot of medical screenings done each day at MEPS, so during your visit you will spend a lot of time waiting. Remember to be patient and respectful. Bring a book or magazine to keep yourself occupied.

Talking with an Air Force Liaison

In addition to the Department of Defense personnel (doctors, nurses, testing staff, etc.) working at MEPS, there are also representatives from each branch of the service. The Air Force liaisons at MEPS are there to help you if you need them. While you should have your recruiter's phone number and other contact information with you just in case, the Air Force liaison will be the first point of contact for any issues you encounter during your visit. He or she can help clear up any problems, fill out paperwork, find needed documents, etc.

The liaison is also the person you will talk to after you complete your medical screening. He or she will go back over *everything* with you again — starting with your enlistment application, going through your medical, educational, and legal histories, and finishing up with any missing information. Though this repetition of information you already organized might seem annoying to you, it is the military's way of making sure that only the best personnel are enlisted. Your talk with the liaison is the chance to make sure that all parts of your application are accurate, so, one more time, DO NOT LIE. Make sure all information is correct and, if not, make sure the corrections are made. The liaison will be making sure you are fingerprinted and that a background check is done, so any discrepancies will be discovered.

Job Selection

Before you head to MEPS, your recruiter will talk to you about job selection, so you should have a good idea of the types of jobs you are interested in when you get to the meeting with your Air Force liaison. The basic Air Force jobs are outlined in Chapter 7, but your recruiter can give you more details about specific jobs within each category. Keep an open mind about your job options. Your ASVAB scores may reveal that you have an aptitude for a career field you hadn't previously considered.

Your recruiter can help you think about the jobs that are available to you. He or she can offer tips and suggestions. In addition, see if you can talk with Airmen who are doing the jobs you are considering. Do they like their jobs? What other jobs would they recommend you look at? The Air Force does have job services support in place, so if you decide later on in your career (usually after your first term of service) that you'd rather be working in intelligence than in air traffic control, you have the option to retake the ASVAB and try to qualify for a new Military Occupational Specialty (MOS)—aka job.

After you have completed your physicals at MEPS and taken the ASVAB (if you have not already taken it), then you will head to a meeting with an Air Force liaison, where you make your job selection and finalize your contract. Liaisons have a computer system, which tells them, up-to-the-minute, which jobs are open and which you are qualified for, based on your ASVAB scores (or based on the scores you are likely to get, as determined by the mini version of the ASVAB taking in your recruiter's office, if you haven't taken the full test yet), what you are personally interested in doing, your ability to get needed security clearance(s), your ability to pass physical requirements, etc. By the end of the process, you will have a temporary assignment for the MOS you want. That assignment will tell the Air Force when you need to leave for basic training, based on when your school for your MOS will begin. That information is added to your contract and you will now know your scheduled departure date for basic training.

Oath of Enlistment

After you have successfully completed the ASVAB, the medical tests, and the meeting with your Air Force liaison and all personnel have determined that there are no further issues which will prevent you from enlisting in the Air Force, then you are ready to take the Oath of Enlistment. This will be the first of two Oaths you take. This Oath of Enlistment installs you into the Delayed Entry Program in an inactive reserve status. The second Oath will be taken the day you leave for basic training and it will install you into the active duty military. (If you are enlisting into the reserves, then you will only take the Oath

Taking the Oath of Enlistment is the last part of your visit to Military Entrance Processing Station (DoD Photographer).

once. As soon as you take it, you are a member of the military and the reserves.)

The Oath of Enlistment is a serious, solemn occasion. You should not take it lightly. If, after going through processing at MEPS and talking with your recruiter and Air Force liaison, you have any doubts at all about enlisting, then do not take the Oath. It is better to temporarily disappoint your recruiter than to sign up for something you do not want. Read over the Oath carefully and make sure you are able to agree to it, freely and clearly.

I, _____, do solemnly swear (or affirm) that I will support and defend the Constitution of the United States against all enemies, foreign and domestic; that I will bear true faith and allegiance to the same; and that I will obey the orders of the President of the United States and the orders of the officers appointed over me, according to regulations and the Uniform Code of Military Justice. So help me God.

The Oath is administered at MEPS by military officers. Your family is welcome to attend and to take photographs afterward. If for some reason they cannot attend, MEPS or your recruiter can often stage the Oath at a later time so that they can take pictures then.

After the Oath

After you have sworn the Oath, you will return to the Air Force liaison to verify your paperwork. He or she will congratulate you on your decision to enlist in the Air Force and will instruct you on proper behavior during your time in the Delayed Entry Program. Make sure you get his or her contact information, so that you can get in touch with them if needed. Then you can head home.

Your recruiter will receive your paperwork and should call you within a day or two of your return from MEPS. If he or she doesn't call, you should call and schedule a time to go over your paperwork again. Any problems or errors *must* be corrected before you leave for basic training, so it is crucial that you proofread your documents as many times as you can. You will also need to schedule a time to talk with your recruiter about what you can do to prepare for basic training during your time in the Delayed Entry Program. Chapter 15 has some basic tips for how to get ready.

Taking the Armed Services Vocational Aptitude Battery

One of the basic requirements of enlistment is the Armed Services Vocational Aptitude Battery test or the ASVAB. The ASVAB gives the military an idea of what your skills are and what jobs you might be suited for. In this section we'll look at what the ASVAB is, how it is administered, what tests make up the ASVAB, what the scores mean, and how you can work on improving your scores.

What Is the ASVAB?

The ASVAB is basically a test of your knowledge and skills. The military wants to know what you already know about math, science, language, electronics, mechanics, and more, and it wants to know what skills — or aptitude — you have for jobs in various fields. By knowing what you are or might be good at, the military can place you in a job where you can succeed. This is good for both you and the military. If you're successful in your job, then you're more likely to be happy and a happy enlistee is one who is more likely to stay in the military.

To test your knowledge and skills, you take the nine tests that are part of the ASVAB. These tests make up the two parts of the ASVAB: the Armed Forces Qualifying Test (or AFQT) and the technical subtests. Nine tests may sound like a lot, but the individual tests are not long and you do not have to master every one of them. The technical subtests are designed to show the military what skills you have, so that they can match you with a job. The AFQT, however, is the part of the test that will determine whether or not you even qualify to enlist in the military, so it is important that you at least do well on those tests.

How Do You Take the ASVAB?

There are several ways you can take the ASVAB. Many high schools will administer the ASVAB to their students. The students can then use their scores to discuss their aptitudes with their guidance counselor. Since the ASVAB is designed to tell you what you are good at or what you may be good at, it is useful as part of a career decision-making process. If you take the ASVAB at your school, your personal information may be shared with recruiters. They can then contact you to tell you more about the opportunities available to you in the military. If you met your recruiter this way, then he or she can use the scores from the ASVAB you took at school to determine both your eligibility to enter the military and the jobs available to you. ASVAB scores are good for two years, so even if you take the ASVAB in high school, but don't decide to enlist until a year after graduation, your scores are still valid.

However, if you did not take the ASVAB in high school, you will have to take it as part of the enlistment process. At the beginning of your time talking to a recruiter, he or she may give you a mini–ASVAB test (called a Computer Adaptive Screening Test [CAST] or an Enlistment Screening Test [EST]) right in the recruiting office. This test will give both you and your recruiter an idea of how you will probably score on the AFQT portion of the ASVAB. If you do well on that mini-test, then you will likely do well on the full ASVAB. (See the section to come on ASVAB scores for more information on how the test is scored and what your scores mean.)

When you go to take the full ASVAB, you will take it at either a Military Entrance Processing Station (MEPS) or a Mobile Examining Team (MET) site. MEPS is a facility that is run by the Department of

Defense (DOD) to assist and streamline military enlistment for all branches of the service. (See Chapter 12 for more information on MEPS.) MET sites exist solely for the purpose of administering the ASVAB. There are two ways of taking the ASVAB: Computer Adaptive Test (CAT) and Paper and Pencil (PAP). Most MEPS facilities only give the CAT and most MET sites only give the PAP. You are tested on the same type of information, regardless of which type of test you take, but the method of testing is fairly different. Though it is more likely you will take the CAT, you should know how to take both types, because you could end up taking the PAP.

COMPUTER ADAPTIVE TEST (CAT)

The CAT is taken on a computer. You will use a mouse to select your answers, though you will have scratch paper provided for working

The Computer Adaptive Test is one way you may take the ASVAB (DoD Photographer).

them out. But the CAT is not just a computer version of the pencil and paper test. Instead it adapts as you answer questions. The first question for each test will be of medium difficulty. If you get it right, then the second question is a little harder, but if you get the first question wrong, then the next one is easier. You cannot, however, choose the order in which you answer questions in order to answer the easier ones first. You have to take the questions as they are given to you.

The entire CAT takes however long as it takes you to finish, though each section has a time limit. Answers are input and then finalized. Once they are finalized, you cannot go back and change them. You keep answering questions until time is up or until you finish the section. Once you finish one section, you move immediately into the next. You cannot go back and check answers on sections you have already finished. You will receive your scores at the end of the test.

PAPER AND PENCIL TEST (PAP)

This is a traditional standardized test, using test booklets and bubble sheets you fill in with pencils. The questions vary in difficulty throughout the test. Within a section, you can answer questions in any order you like, which allows you to quickly answer the easier questions and then go back to the harder ones.

Once a section starts you answer questions until you finish or until time is up. If you finish early, you can go back and check your answers and change them if you need to, but you cannot go on to the next section. The PAP test takes about three to four hours. Your scores are mailed to your recruiter within a few days from when you take the test.

How Many Questions Are on the ASVAB?

The number of questions on the ASVAB depends upon whether you take the CAT or the PAP.

#	Name of Test Questions	Type*	CAT # of Questions	CAT Time	PAP # of Questions	PAP Time
1	General Science	Tech	16	8 mins	25	11 mins
2	Arithmetic Reasoning	AFQT	16	39 mins	30	36 mins
3	Word Knowledge	AFQT	16	8 mins	35	11 mins
4	Paragraph Comprehension	AFQT	11	22 mins	15	13 mins
5	Mathematics Knowledge	AFQT	16	20 mins	25	24 mins
6	Electronics Information	Tech	16	8 mins	20	9 mins
7†	Auto Information Shop Information	Tech	11 11	7 mins 6 mins	25	11 mins
8	Mechanical Comprehension	Tech	16	20 mins	25	19 mins
9	Assembling Objects	Tech	16	16 mins	25	15 mins
	Total:		145	154 mins	225	149 mins

*Tech = Technical.
†Auto and Shop Information is two separate tests on the CAT and one combined test on the PAP.

What Tests Make Up the ASVAB?

Armed Forces Qualifying Test (AFQT)

- Arithmetic Reasoning (AR): Basic word problems based on mathematical situations you might encounter every day. Designed to test your ability to reason and solve problems.
- Mathematics Knowledge (MK): General math problems at a high school level, including algebra and geometry. Designed to test your knowledge of mathematics.
- Paragraph Comprehension (PC): You will read paragraphs and answer questions based on what you read. Designed to test your ability to analyze written material.

- Word Knowledge (WK): Questions about the meanings and use of words. Designed to test your vocabulary and communication skills.

TECHNICAL TESTS

- Assembling Objects (AO): You are shown drawings of objects and must answer questions about how they fit together. Designed to test your ability to use spatial reasoning.
- Automotive and Shop Information (AS): Quizzes you on automobile mechanics, tools, shop terminology, uses of parts, etc. Designed to see what you know about mechanics and mechanical work.
- Electronics Information (EI): Questions about circuits, electrical systems, electronics terminology, radio principles, etc. Designed to see what you know about electronics and working with electrical and radio components.
- General Science (GS): Basic science questions — life, physical, earth — at a high school level. Designed to test your knowledge of science.
- Mechanical Comprehension (MC): Tests you on mechanical and physical science principles. Designed to see what you know about how machines work, how mechanics affect real life, etc.

What Do the ASVAB Scores Mean?

There is no overall score on the ASVAB. Instead, there are two separate groups of scores which are important: your AFQT percentile and your composite scores.

THE AFQT PERCENTILE

The AFQT percentile is what determines your eligibility to enlist. It is derived by this formula: 2(VE) + AR + MK. That means that your scores from Paragraph Comprehension (PC) and Word Knowledge

(WK) are combined to create a Verbal Expression score. That score is then added to your Arithmetic Reasoning (AR) and Mathematics Knowledge (MK) scores to give your AFQT raw score. The raw score is compared to the scores of ASVAB test takers who participated in a study in 1997. That comparison allows the test to determine your AFQT percentile. So, if your AFQT percentile is 53, that means that your raw score was better than 53 percent of the test takers in that study.

The military divides the AFQT scores into categories, which are then used to determine a potential enlistee's eligibility. When the military's recruitment goals are lowered (meaning they don't need as many personnel) or when there are more people applying for enlistment than needed, then they usually raise the acceptable AFQT scores for potential enlistees to make sure they are only bringing in the best recruits.

Category	AFQT Percentiles	Category	AFQT Percentiles
Category I	100–93	Category IVA	30–21*
Category II	92–65	Category IVB	20–16*
Category IIIA	64–50	Category IVC	15–10*
Category IIIB	49–31	Category V	9–0†

Any potential enlistees in Category IV must have a high school diploma, not a GED. Also, only 20 percent of enlistees in the entire military can be from Category IV.

†You are not eligible to enlist in the military if you are in Category V.

Each branch of the military has a different minimum AFQT score. As of September 2010, those were:

Branch	Minimum AFQT w/HS Diploma	Minimum AFQT w/GED	Notes about GED Holders
Air Force	36	65	The Air Force allows less than 1 percent of its yearly enlistees to have GEDs. GED holders who have 15 or more college credits are considered the same as those with high school diplomas.

Branch	Minimum AFQT w/HS Diploma	Minimum AFQT w/GED	Notes about GED Holders
Army	31	50	The Army only allows 15 percent of its yearly enlistees to hold a GED. GED holders who have 15 or more college credits are considered the same as those with high school diplomas.
Coast Guard	45 — and your scores must qualify you for A Schools (training after basic	45 — and your scores must qualify you for A Schools (training after basic)	The Coast Guard has very tight limits on the number of GED holders it accepts. Anyone wanting to enlist in the Coast Guard with a GED must also have completed 15 or more college credits.
Marine Corps	31	50	The Marine Corps allows less than 5 percent of its yearly enlistees to have GEDs. GED holders who have 15 or more college credits are considered the same as those with high school diplomas.
Navy	35	50	Very few GED holders are allowed into the Navy and those that are must not have any issues requiring a waiver. GED holders who have 15 or more college credits are considered the same as those with high school diplomas.

COMPOSITE SCORES

Your composite scores are what determine which jobs you are eligible for. Each branch of the military has a different way of calculating those scores and determining which scores go with which military job. For the current information on how each branch calculates its composite scores and which scores go with which job, visit *http://usmilitary.about.com/od/joiningthemilitary/a/asvabjob.htm* or check out the latest edition of Rod Power's *ASVAB for Dummies* (Wiley Publishing), which has information on which subtests correspond to which military job.

Retaking the ASVAB

If you do not score well enough on the AFQT portion of the ASVAB to qualify for enlistment, you can retake the ASVAB, but not right away. You have to wait thirty days to retake the ASVAB a second time and then wait six months to retake it a third time. Your most recent score is the one which is used to determine your eligibility. Each branch of the military, though, has limits on whether or not you can retake the ASVAB simply to increase your scores in order to qualify for a particular job or enlistment bonus or for a reason other than having an AFQT percentile that is too low for enlistment. Your recruiter can give you the most up-to-date information on his or her branch's restrictions.

The best thing you can do to improve your scores is to brush up on your basic math, science, and vocabulary skills. A high AFQT will open up opportunities for you in the military. You'll be more likely to qualify for waivers (if needed), to qualify for enlistment bonuses, and to qualify for other incentives. Also, because your ASVAB scores remain valid while you are a member of the military, you can use them later on to qualify for advanced training or reclassification into a different job field, though they are not used to determine promotions or awards.

Studying for the ASVAB

Your first step should be go purchase an ASVAB study guide. You can also check them out from the public library or your school or college library, but there may be long waiting lists and you will not be able to write in the library's copy. If you prefer to practice online, check to see if your public library or school or college library has access to an online test prep program. They might and, if so, it will be free to use. Or, to work on your math, science, and language skills, you can use March 2 Success, a free online test preparation program sponsored by the United States Army. You can sign up here: *https://www.march2success.com*. (Using the site does not obligate you to enlist in the Army and they do not share your information with Army recruiters.) March 2 Success does not have a specific ASVAB practice test, but it offers programs to help you boost your basic skills.

Take the sample tests in the study guide or online. They will show you what areas you need improvement in. Then focus your study to those areas. The ASVAB is testing science, math, and vocabulary on a high school level, so if you have been out of school for a time or if you have a subject you were not as good at, then you'll definitely need to brush up your skills.

Though the study guide or online program will have a lot of questions and several sample tests, you should not assume that the questions on the sample tests are the same as those that will be on the actual ASVAB. The ASVAB questions are closely guarded and no study guides—either in print or online—will have access to them. Instead the study guide questions are meant to give you an idea of what type of questions will be on the actual ASVAB and what areas you need to improve in.

Study Tips

- *Be sure to study in a quiet place with good lighting and a firm surface for writing.* Music is okay, if it's not so loud that it distracts you, though you're probably better off sticking with instrumental music, rather than songs with lyrics.

- *Make sure you have all the supplies you need before you begin studying.* Pencils and scratch paper are vital, but you should not have a calculator around to tempt you as you will not be able to use one on the test.

- *Include a stopwatch or a clock so that you can time yourself.* When you take practice tests, you'll want to be sure that you mimic testing conditions, including time limits.

- *Study in longer blocks.* You'll want to set aside an hour or two for each study session. That will allow you the time to focus and absorb information.

- *While occasional study groups can be helpful, make sure you mostly study by yourself.* You won't have anyone to rely on when you take the test, so you need to be sure you can do it on your own.

- *Take notes during your study sessions.* Taking clear notes will help you remember information. Besides, you'll have to take notes in your classes during basic training, so you might as well practice that skill now!

- *Set goals for what you want to accomplish and when.* Your main goal is to do as well as you can on the ASVAB, but also have smaller goals that will help you focus and give you a feeling of accomplishment. Small goals are a good way of breaking your studying into more manageable chunks. You could set a small goal for how much you want to cover in a particular study session or week.

- *Continue practicing even when you aren't studying.* The best way to improve your math and verbal scores is to use your skills all day, every day.
  - *Read the newspaper and a wide variety of books.* Even reading books that are light and fun will help you improve your vocabulary. As you are reading, jot down words you don't know and then look them up in a dictionary. Write down the definition and then make sure to use that word in conversation some time that same day.

o *Use mental math whenever possible.* Rather than reaching for a calculator, do the problem in your head while you're shopping, out to eat, paying bills, etc. Doing quick math problems in your mind or on paper will keep your math skills sharp.

Preparing for the Test

- *Get plenty of sleep the night before.* Don't stay up studying. Last minute cramming will not put the information into your brain and it might interfere with the information you already know.
- *Eat a light breakfast with some protein (eggs, bacon, etc.).* That will help you keep from getting hungry during the test. Have a glass of water to drink, but don't overdo it. You don't want to have to go to the bathroom in the middle of the test.
- *Assemble your supplies the night before.* Your photo ID, pencils and scratch paper are the most important. Bring your glasses, even if you wear contacts. Wear a watch (with a second hand if possible) to help keep track of time.
- *Get to the testing site early.* You'll want to be there at least fifteen minutes before the test starts, so that you can handle any administrative tasks and not feel rushed. Be sure to account for traffic. You might even consider doing a test drive over to the testing facility a day or two before.
- *Reschedule if needed.* If you wake up and feel sick or if you are injured or if you have recently had a stressful event happen, then you won't be at your best to take the test. You can always reschedule. Just call your recruiter and he or she will handle it.

Taking the ASVAB

Your recruiter will arrange the time and location for you to take the ASVAB. He or she will help you work out any transportation issues, such if you need to stay overnight the evening before the test. If you are taking the ASVAB at MEPS, you may be doing it at the same time as your physical, which can make for a long day or couple of days. But whenever and wherever you take the ASVAB, there are some basic strategies which can help you do better on the test.

DURING THE TEST

- *Relax.* It is just a test. If you are calm, then you will automatically do better on it.
- *Listen to or read all instructions carefully.* If you don't understand, ask the person administering the test to explain.
- *Work steadily, but don't rush.* Getting questions correct is more important than the number of questions you get through. You'll want to answer as many questions as possible, but not at the expense of getting questions wrong.
- *Make sure to read every question carefully.* Be sure that you understand what information is being asked for. Then read all of the answer choices provided to you.
- *Think carefully about what you think the answer is.* Then think about it again.
- *Eliminate logically.* Look at the answer choices. In a multiple choice test, two of them are usually obviously wrong. That leaves two that are possibilities. Choose the one that you think is the best possible answer.
- *If your answer does not match any of the answer choices, then look back over the question.* See if you need to think about things in a different way or look at the answer in a different direction.
- *When in doubt, guess.* As long as you have eliminated some of the answer choices logically, then if you really do not know, make a guess about one of the two remaining choices. You are not penalized for wrong answers; you just don't get a point for them.

Your recruiter is always the best person to ask about the ASVAB. He or she knows the most up-to-date information about the ASVAB and can walk you through the process of studying for it, taking it, and understanding your scores. When you've done the best you can do on the ASVAB, the scores will not only assist you in the enlistment process, but will also reveal more about your career skills. Taking the ASVAB will teach you more about who you are and what careers you might enjoy.

14

Joining the Delayed Entry Program

Unlike in the past, when you might have gone to MEPS, done your testing and physical, signed your papers, and left for basic training the next day, nowadays almost every single person who joins the military enters into the Delayed Entry Program (DEP) first. It is extremely rare to leave for basic training any sooner than two weeks after visiting MEPS and most enlistees spend six weeks or more in DEP before departing for training. The military uses the DEP because it allows them to better manage their numbers, spreading out new recruits evenly throughout the year. The branches of the military have set numbers of personnel they have to maintain each year and they need to carefully plan how many personnel are added each week, month, quarter, etc.

The amount of time you spend in the DEP depends on many factors. When your liaison helps you pick your job while you are at MEPS, he or she will know when there will be an opening in the school to train you for that job. They count back nine weeks from that date to account for your time in basic training and that gives them the date you will leave for training. That date can be up to 365 days from the time you took the Oath of Enlistment to enter the DEP. And that's good news, because the time you spend in DEP is time you have to prepare for basic training. By getting yourself ready — physically, mentally, educationally, financially — you will set yourself up for success in basic training. The more preparation you have, the better you will do during training.

Behavior in the DEP

Unless you are enlisting in the reserves, you will not be paid during your time in the DEP. (Reserve enlistees can begin attending training sessions with their unit even before attending basic and will be paid for their time.) Instead you are a member of the inactive reserves until you ship off to basic. Even though you are not being paid, you still have work to do and expectations you must live up to. Your recruiter and the Air Force liaison at MEPS will brief you on those expectations, but it doesn't hurt to go over them here as well.

- *Behave like an Airman.* Your time in DEP should not be spent partying and slacking off. You are expected to uphold the values of the Air Force and to carry yourself as an Airman.
- *Prepare yourself for recruit training.* In the next chapter we will go over all the ways you can set yourself up for success during basic training.
- *Attending any scheduled meetings.* Air Force recruiters set up regular visits with their enlistees where they exercise together, learn basic military and Air Force information, and get a sense of what life will be like as an Airman.
- *Finish school.* If you are still in high school when you enlist, you MUST graduate and you must do so on time. Otherwise you will jeopardize your enlistment and your job assignment.
- *Keep in touch with your recruiter.* Alert him or her to any changes in your situation, from major ones like marriage or legal problems, to minor changes such as changing addresses.

Leaving the DEP

Because you are not a full member of the Air Force during your time in the DEP, you can change your mind about enlisting and leave the DEP with no serious repercussions. HOWEVER, this is a very serious step and should only be taken in extreme situations. You should not go through the stages of the enlistment process — talking to a recruiter, visiting MEPS, taking the Oath of Enlistment — without sober consideration of the decision you are making. By the time you enter the DEP, you should be certain of your choice and eager to prepare for basic training.

But things can happen during your time in the DEP which might cause you to have to change your mind about enlisting. A scholarship to college, the death of a family member, pregnancy, trouble with the law, a serious injury — these are all situations which could arise and prevent you from completing your obligation. The first thing you should do is speak with your recruiter and you should do that as soon as you realize there is a problem. Schedule a time to speak privately and inform him or her of your situation calmly and rationally.

You should know that your recruiter will try very hard to keep you from leaving the Air Force. By this point in the process the Air Force has spent a lot of time and money getting you approved to enlist. They feel that you will be an asset to the Air Force and they aren't going to want to lose you. Your recruiter will try to come up with other options to help you out, such as changing your ship date, getting you approved for a college Recruit Officer Training Corps (ROTC) program, etc. But if your reasons are valid and solid and there is no way you can enlist because of your situation, then they will have to approve your request. You may have to write a letter to the Air Force Recruiting Service outlining your reasons for leaving the DEP. The address is in the "For More Information" section in the back of this book.

If your situation is temporary — an injury or a family emergency, for example — and you still want to enlist in the Air Force at a later date, then you will likely be able to, though you might need a waiver to do so. Tell your recruiter if you think that might be the case, so that he or she can help you out. But if you are just experiencing "buyer's remorse" and you want to leave the DEP because you no longer want to be an Airman, then you will more than likely not be considered to be a good candidate for enlistment if you change your mind again in the future. So think carefully before making any decision.

Using the DEP to Prepare for Recruit Training

The best thing you can do during your time in the DEP is to prepare to leave for basic training. You can get yourself in the best possible shape, which will make your time in recruit training easier. The next section has information on how you can prepare mentally and physically.

Preparing for Basic Training

All enlistees worry about basic training. They wonder if they'll be able to keep up physically; they stress about being away from friends and family; they aren't sure how they'll cope with being ordered about all day. Unfortunately the only way to know how you're going to do in basic training is to go through it. Everyone's basic training experience is different, so there is no way to prepare for all the fears, stresses, and hardships you'll face. But the Delayed Entry Program gives you the time to prepare to face *most* of those fears, stresses, and hardships. If you work hard before you leave for basic, then you'll be ready to work hard during basic, which is what will make you a successful recruit.

There are four ways you should prepare yourself for basic training: physically, mentally, socially, and emotionally. Each of these is as important as the others. By working on them all, you'll insure that you have the best possible start to your basic training experience.

Physical Preparation

Because the physical fitness portion of basic training is what worries enlistees the most and because poor physical fitness sets you up for failure during basic training, physical training is the first aspect of preparation you should focus on. If you are in good physical condition when you leave for basic training, you will find yourself with one less worry during your time there. Your recruiter will give you guidelines for how to get yourself in shape for basic training and he or she may even exercise with you, but ultimately you are responsible for your own physical conditioning.

Getting in shape now will mean that you are ready for the intense physical exercise during basic training (Official U.S. Air Force photograph by Melinda Mueller).

STARTING AN EXERCISE ROUTINE

The first thing you should do before beginning any exercise routine is to consult with your family physician. MEPS should have caught any serious medical problems, but your doctor should still check you out to make sure you are physically ready for an exercise program. A checkup will also help to catch any physical problems which could delay you when you get to basic training. You don't want to get all the way to training and then discover that you aren't in good enough shape to start!

If you can afford to, joining a gym or a YMCA is a good idea. The staff there can help you plan an exercise program which meets your needs, fits your body, and will get you ready in the time you have. But if you cannot afford a gym, you can still prepare on your own. The Air Force has a factsheet which will walk you through the process of getting in shape. It can be found at *http://www.basictraining.af.mil/library/*

factsheets/factsheet.asp?id=15719. You can also check your public, school, or college library for books on exercise and look for exercise plans on the internet. If you are still in high school, talk to your gym teacher or ROTC instructor about helping you plan a workout program. Or, if you are no longer in high school, check with a local college to see if they offer a degree in physical education. If so, talk to one of the professors and see if they would consider giving a student extra credit if they plan a training regimen for you.

Important things to remember as you set up an exercise program:

- *Vary your exercises.* Only focusing on running will not help you develop a healthy level of physical fitness. Be sure that you include all three of these activities:
  o Flexibility exercises (which prevent injury): warm-up and cool-down stretches
  o Cardiorespiratory workouts (which increase your heart rate and improve breathing): running (outdoors is best; don't just run on a treadmill), swimming, biking, rollerblading, active sports
  o Muscular strength activities (which help build muscle): sit-ups/crunches, push-ups, pull-ups (or flexed arm hangs for women), working out on exercise machines or with weights
- *Start slowly.* If you fling yourself immediately into a hard training regimen, you will get injured. Injuries, either during the DEP or during basic, will delay your training which could affect your job training placement, thereby affecting your ability to get the job you want. A severe enough injury could even prevent you from becoming an Airman.
- *Be consistent.* Work out three to five times a week for 45 minutes to an hour at a time. Try to work out at the same time each day so that your body gets used to the routine.
- *Be patient.* If you cannot run a mile when you start training, that's okay. That is why you are training. Start by walking, then add in jogging, gradually increasing the amount of jog-

ging and decreasing the amount of walking. Before you know it, you'll be running!

- *Gradually progress.* Add a little on to your workout each week, not so much as to overload your body, but enough to make sure you are consistently challenged.
- *Aim for endurance, not speed.* Though you will have some timed runs during basic training, most of the runs and hikes you will do will focus on endurance. During your preparations you should start out with longer, slower runs. This will allow you to build up the lung and muscle strength to go the distance when needed. As you train, you will find that you are able to add more miles into the same amount of time.
- *Watch your form.* You'll want to learn the correct, Air Force way of doing sit-ups and push-ups, so that you do not waste your practice. Your recruiter can help you practice.
    - *Push-ups*: Start with your hands under your shoulders, arms straight, feet together or up to 12 inches apart behind you, toes curled under. Lower down until your arms make a 90 degree angle, then push back up until your arms are straight again. Your body should stay in one line while you do a push-up.
    - *Crunches*: Lie on your back with your feet flat on the floor, knees bent. Fold your arms across your chest and keep them there with no gaps while you do crunches. Raise your upper body until your forearms or elbows touch your thighs and then lower your body back down until your shoulder blades touch the floor again. You may not lift your rear end off of the floor. A friend can hold your feet for you, if needed.
- *Set a goal.* When you get to Air Force basic training, you will take an initial Physical Fitness Test (PFT). This test tells the Air Force if you are in shape enough to handle the rigors of basic training. If you cannot pass the initial PFT, you will not be considered in good physical condition for basic training and will likely be sent home.

    The Air Force has suggestions for what your training goals

should be as you work out. Those goals are mid-way between the initial PFT standards and the requirements to pass the final PFT, which is taken towards the end of basic training. If you train towards the Air Force's suggestions or towards the final PFT while you in the DEP, then you will definitely pass the initial test. You take the initial PFT in your first days of basic training, when you will still be suffering from culture shock and under a lot of stress, so you want to aim to be able to do more than the test requires anyway. That way you will ensure that you are able to easily pass the test when you take it in those stressful conditions. By aiming towards the final PFT, you will be able to accomplish that goal easily.

Here are the initial PFT requirements, the graduation requirements, and what the Air Force suggests you aim for:

Event	Initial PFT Minimum— Men	Final PFT Minimum— Men	Air Force Training Goal—Men
Run	1.5 mile run in 18 min. 30 sec.	1.5 mile run in 11 min. 57 sec.	1.5 mile run in 13 min. 45 sec.
Push-ups (in 2 min.)	5	33	25
Sit-ups (in 2 min.)	10	42	35

Event	Initial PFT Minimum— Women	Final PFT Minimum— Women	Air Force Training Goal—Women
Run	1.5 mile run in 21 min. 35 sec.	1.5 mile run in 14 min. 26 sec.	1.5 mile run in 16 min.
Push-ups (in 2 min.)	3	18	15
Sit-ups (in 2 min.)	5	38	30

For more information, you can check out the Air Force's "Are You Ready for Basic Training?" factsheet, available online here: *http://www.basictraining.af.mil/library/factsheets/factsheet.asp?id=15718.*

- *Stay alert to prevent injury.* Pay attention to what your body tells you. Muscle soreness is normal when starting an exercise routine, but if it seems extreme or if you injure yourself, visit your doctor immediately. Minor problems can become major ones if left untreated.
- *Dress the part.* Proper workout attire will help prevent injuries.
  - Wear clothes that are appropriate to the weather. Avoid plastic suits designed to make you sweat, even if you need to lose weight. These will cause you to overheat and get sick.
  - Wear shoes that work for your feet. Good running shoes don't have to be expensive, but they do need to be properly fitted. Go to a store that specializes in running shoes and get the associates there to assist you in finding the right shoes.
- *Work out with a friend.* You are more likely to maintain and succeed in an exercise program if you have someone to support you. Working out with a fellow enlistee, your recruiter, a friend, or a parent is a great way to get in shape and enjoy yourself at the same time.
- *Have fun.* Exercise can be fun if you allow yourself to enjoy it. In addition to working on the running, sit-ups, and push-ups you'll need to pass the initial PFT when you get to basic training, treat yourself to a fun exercise once a week. Join a team sport, take a dance or aerobics class, go for a hike or a bike ride, etc. These treats can keep you interested and engaged in your exercise program.

OTHER PHYSICAL PREPARATION

Besides working out, you'll also want to prepare your body in other ways. By leaving for basic training with the healthiest body possible, you'll be less likely to get sick while you're there.

- *Eat right.* If you haven't already been eating a healthy diet, now is the time to start. Your physician can help you learn more about which foods you should be eating and which you should cut back on. You can also visit the Department of Agriculture's healthy eating website *http://www.choosemyplate.gov* for more information.

There are a few easy changes you can make which will help your transition to the dining facilities at basic training.

- *Cut out fast food and sodas and cut back on desserts.* You won't have access to them (or only very limited access), so you might as well get used to doing without now.
- *Learn to eat quickly and quietly.* Try to eat two of your meals a day in just 10–15 minutes each without talking to anyone, which is about what you'll be doing at basic training.
- *Drink water.* Water is better than anything else you can drink, including milk, juice, or sports drinks. Try to drink at least eight 8-ounce glasses a day.
- *Eat a balanced meal.* Make sure you include plenty of fruits and vegetables and that you aren't just eating meat and starches (like bread or potatoes).

• *Lose weight sensibly.* You will need to be below 20 percent body fat for men and 28 percent for women in order to attend Air Force basic training. Your recruiter will tell you if you are not at the proper weight. But be sure to lose weight slowly and carefully. No matter how much you need to lose overall, you should never lose more than 1 to 2 pounds per week. Do not go on a crash diet to lose weight, because you will only rebound later and gain the weight back. Instead learn to eat low fat, healthy meals and be sure to exercise (especially aerobic exercise) regularly.

• *Stop smoking and drinking.* You will not be able to smoke or drink while you are in basic training. Quitting now will not only help you during training, it will also improve your health and make sure you are in good shape before you leave. (It should go without saying that you aren't doing illegal drugs and that you aren't drinking or smoking if you are underage.)

• *Change your sleeping habits.* While in basic you will get up very

early every day, often as early as 4 or 4:30 A.M., though sometimes earlier than that. Now is the time to learn how. Start
going to bed around 9 or 10 P.M. and getting up between 4:30
and 5 A.M.

   If you live in a location that is in a different time zone from
San Antonio, Texas (which is where Air Force basic training
takes place), it is a good idea to start adjusting to that time
zone about one or two weeks before you leave. For example,
San Antonio is on Central Time. If you live in Wyoming
(which is on Mountain time), then you are going to want to go
to bed between 8 and 9 P.M. (Mountain time) and get up
between 3:30 and 4 A.M. (Mountain time).

- *Toughen your feet.* Start walking in boots now and you will be
  better prepared for walking in them at basic training. You can
  use hiking boots if you have them or get a pair of military
  boots from a military surplus store. Just make sure that your
  boots fit properly and that you do not run in them. (Almost all
  running in basic training is done in athletic shoes.)

- *Practice proper hygiene.* Basic training means living in close quarters with other people and that means you'll be more likely to
  get sick, even though the personnel at basic training do their
  very best to prevent illnesses. If you make it a habit to wash
  your hands often, especially before eating and after coughing,
  sneezing or going to the restroom, then you will decrease your
  chance of illness.

- *Learn to swim.* Though you do not have to know how to swim to
  join the Air Force and you are not required to qualify in
  swimming during basic training, it is always a good idea to
  learn. Your time in the Air Force will take you to a variety of
  locales and you never know when needing swimming skills will
  come in handy. Additionally, swimming is excellent cardiopul-
  monary exercise which will get you in shape for basic training.

- *Practice safe sex.* If you get pregnant during your time in the DEP,
  you will not be allowed to go to basic training. If your wife or

girlfriend gets pregnant, then it can also cause complications for you. The Air Force will not let you leave basic training to attend the birth, and more than likely won't let you leave your follow on training either. You will also have to work out how you are going to help support your child while you are still only a junior enlisted Airman. Additionally, all recruits are tested for sexually transmitted diseases when they arrive at basic. Being diagnosed with one will more than likely get you sent back home.

- *Avoid injuries, body modifications, drug use, etc.* Drive carefully. Don't take silly physical risks. Do not get a new tattoo or body piercing. Do not use illegal drugs and check with your recruiter to be sure that any new prescription drugs will not disqualify you.

Mental/Educational Preparation

FINISHING SCHOOL

If you are still in high school when you enlist in the Air Force, then the most important thing you can do during the DEP is to finish school. If you do not graduate, then you will not be allowed to leave for basic training. You don't have to make straight As, but you should work hard, study carefully, ask your teachers for help if you need it, and stay out of trouble. If it looks like you might not graduate or if another school related problem, such as a suspension, arises, alert your recruiter immediately.

KEEPING YOUR BRAIN SHARP

A smart Airman is a good Airman. Just as you work out to keep your body healthy, you want to work your mind to keep it healthy. Basic training isn't just about physical education. There is a lot of learning that will take place during your nine weeks and you want to get your mind ready to soak it all in. Here are some tips for brain workouts:

- *Practice taking notes.* There will be classes in classrooms and on the field during basic training and you will be tested on what you learn. You'll want to be able to take effective notes even when you are tired. The public library will have books on note taking or you can check out the resources at *http://www.college-board.com/student/plan/college-success/955.html.*
- *Turn off the TV and reduce computer and videogame time.* You will not have access to a television, computer, or videogames while you are at basic training. Start getting used to that now by making them an occasional treat, rather than an everyday habit. Use the extra time to work out, visit with friends and family, read, or learn military skills in advance.
- *Work on math skills.* If you do not feel that your mathematics skills are where you want them to be, now is the time to work on them. No matter what your job in the Air Force, you will use math. The public library will have books on math to help you brush up. One easy way to improve is to stop using a calculator and do all math problems in your head or by hand on paper.
- *Read.* The best thing you can do to improve your mind is to read. The Air Force has a Chief of Staff Professional Reading List which is updated every year. The current list and lists from past years can be found at *http://www.af.mil/information/csaf reading/index.asp.*

The 2012 Chief of Staff Air Force Professional Reading List is:

- *Paradise Beneath Her Feet: How Women Are Transforming the Middle East* by Isobel Coleman [non-fiction]
- *The Forever War* by Dexter Filkins [non-fiction]
- *Airpower for Strategic Effect* by Colin S. Gray [non-fiction]
- *Why Success Always Starts with Failure* by Tim Harford [non-fiction]
- *Catch-22* by Joseph Heller [fiction]
- *Unbroken: A World War II Story of Survival, Resilience, and Redemption* by Laura Hillenbrand [non-fiction]

- *Physics of the Future: How Science Will Shape Human Destiny and Our Daily Lives by 2100* by Michio Kaku [non-fiction]
- *The Party: The Secret World of China's Communist Leaders* by Richard McGregor [non-fiction]
- *A Country of Vast Designs: James K. Polk, the Mexican War, and the Conquest of the American Continent* by Robert W. Merry [non-fiction]
- *The Words We Live By: Your Annotated Guide to the Constitution* by Linda R. Monk [non-fiction]
- *Freedom Flyers: The Tuskegee Airmen of World War II* by J. Todd Moye [non-fiction]
- *The Hunters: A Novel* by James Salter [fiction]
- *Start with Why: How Great Leaders Inspire Everyone to Take Action* by Simon Sinek [non-fiction]

THINGS TO LEARN IN ADVANCE

You will learn a lot during recruit training; that is what your nine weeks there are for — learning. But there are things you can go ahead and start learning before you even leave for recruit training. Learning these things in advance will save you the trouble of having to learn them while you are tired, sore, and stressed. Some of the things you can learn are specific to the Air Force and will help you understand more about its culture and values. Other items are general to all branches of the military and will be used by you on a daily basis while you are serving in the Air Force. All of these things will be taught to you again while you are at recruit training, but learning them now will save you some brainpower in the future.

Information specific to the Air Force

Air Force Birthday. The Air Force's birthday is September 18, 1947.

Air Force Chain of Command. The chain of command tells you who reports to whom. The chain starts at the top with the President of the United States and works its way down to the person directly in charge of you. (The members of the Department of Defense are always civilians.) You will be expected to know the chain of command as it applies to you — title, rank (if applicable), and name of each person — but you will not know the names of some personnel until you get to basic training. Below is the Air Force chain of command listed in order.

- Commander-in-Chief (aka, the President of the United States)
- Secretary of Defense
- Secretary of the Air Force
- Air Force Chief of Staff
- Air Education and Training Command
- Commander, 37th Training Wing
- Vice Commander, 37th Training Wing
- Commander, 737rd Training Group
- Vice Commander, 737rd Training Group
- Squadron Commander
- First Sergeant
- Training Superintendent
- Section Supervisor
- Team Chief
- Training Instructor(s)
- Recruit

Air Force Core Values. Each branch of the military has its own core values. These are the qualities that they feel are most important for their members to focus on. During recruit training these values are studied extensively and during a service member's career they are expected to live up to these qualities.

The Air Force's core values are "Integrity first, Service before self, and Excellence in all we do."

- *Integrity first* means that Airmen are honest and truthful. They always do the right thing even when no one is watching. They are courageous and fair.
- *Service before self* means that Airmen put their professional

responsibilities before their personal interests. They respect others, follow rules, and practice self-control.

- *Excellence in all we do* means that Airmen strive for the best in their job, in themselves, and in their community.

Air Force Symbol. The Air Force's symbol is the newest of all of the military symbols and emblems. It is the result of six years of work to design a new emblem which represented both the past and the present of the Air Force, as well as the many different elements that are a part of the Air Force.

- The upper part of the symbol — the "wings" — stands for the enlisted men and women of the Air Force. The wings' sharp angles represent swiftness and power. The six sections of the wings stand for the six distinctive capabilities of the Air Force: air and space superiority, global attack, rapid global mobility, precision engagement, information superiority, and agile combat support.
- The sphere in the lower half represents the Earth and stands for the Air Force's vision: "Global Vigilance, Reach, and Power."
- The area around the sphere is a star. That stands for several things. The five points of the star represent the five parts of the Air

The Air Force Symbol (Courtesy U.S. Air Force).

Force family: active-duty Airmen, civilians (both those working for the Air Force and family members), Air National Guard
members, Air Force reserve members, and retirees. The star
also stands for space, one of the areas in which the Air Force
operates. And, finally, the star stands for Air Force officers.

- The three diamonds below the star stand for the three core values
  of "integrity first," "service before self," and "excellence in all
  we do."
- The whole symbol has two meanings. It looks like an eagle, the
  symbol of the United States, but it also looks like a medal, the
  symbol of military valor in service to the United States.

Air Force History. One of the aspects of Air Force recruit training
is learning about the Airmen in whose footsteps you will follow. You
will find out who they were, when they fought, and what their accom-
plishments were. This is important so that you understand how the Air
Force has evolved into the force it is today. Since you will be tested on
this knowledge while you are in basic training, you should read up on
the history of the Air Force before you leave for recruit training. Chapter
6 has a basic overview of the history of the Air Force and you can find
suggestions for books and websites in the "For More Information" section in the back of the book.

The Air Force Song. The U.S. Air Force Song is the official song of
the Air Force. It was written in 1939 by Robert MacArthur Crawford
and was originally called *The Army Air Corps,* as the Air Force was not
yet a separate military branch. Crawford's song was selected from over
700 entries in a contest to write a song for the Army's new Air Corps.
The music can be downloaded from the Air Force Band's website:
http://www.usafband.af.mil/recordings/index.asp. You will be expected
to memorize at least the first verse.

> *Off we go into the wild blue yonder,*
> *Climbing high into the sun;*
> *Here they come zooming to meet our thunder,*
> *At 'em boys, Give 'er the gun!*
> *Down we dive, spouting our flame from under*

Off with one hell of a roar!
We live in fame or go down in flame.
Nothing can stop the U.S. Air Force!

Minds of men fashioned a crate of thunder,
Sent it high into the blue;
Hands of men blasted the world asunder;
How they lived God only knew! (God only knew!)
Souls of men dreaming of skies to conquer
Gave us wings, ever to soar!
With scouts before and bombers galore.
Nothing'll stop the U.S. Air Force!

Here's a toast to the host
Of those who love the vastness of the sky,
To a friend we send a message of his brother men who fly.
We drink to those who gave their all of old,
Then down we roar to score the rainbow's pot of gold.
A toast to the host of men we boast, the U.S. Air Force!

Air Force Motto. The Air Force's motto is "Aim High ... Fly-Fight-Win."

Air Force Organization. The Air Force is organized into units, listed from smallest to largest, though some units are only used for certain occasions, missions, or tasks:

- *Flight:* the smallest Air Force unit; usually made up of anywhere from a dozen airmen to 100 airmen
- *Squadron:* the basic unit of the Air Force; made up of two or more flights
- *Group:* two or more squadrons
- *Wing:* made up of one or more groups
- *Numbered/Named Air Force (NAF):* a group that is usually only used in wartime to organize other units geographically
- *Major Command (MAJCOM):* a major subdivision of the Air Force which is responsible for a large mission
- *Direct Reporting Unit (DRU):* a large group that handles missions that are not covered by MAJCOM

- *Field Operating Agency (FOA):* handles missions that DRU and MAJCOM do not
- *Headquarters United States Air Force:* the main command of the Air Force

Air Force Rank Structure. Rank structure is what tells you the level a military member has reached in the organization. You will be able to tell someone's rank by the markings on their uniform.

Before you leave for training, you should at least learn the rank insignia for the Air Force, though it is a good idea to go ahead and learn about the rank structures for all branches of the military. During your time in the Air Force, you will interact with personnel from all five branches, so if you know the other services' rank insignia as well, then you're ahead of the game.

The enlisted and officer ranks for all five branches of the military are shown on pages 147 and 148.

Airman's Creed. The Airman's Creed was introduced by General T. Michael Moseley, Chief of Staff of the Air Force, on April 25, 2007. It was written as part of the Air Force's new focus on training all Airmen to be warriors. You will learn the creed in basic training and be expected to live by it.

> *I am an American Airman.*
> *I am a Warrior.*
> *I have answered my Nation's call.*
>
> *I am an American Airman.*
> *My mission is to Fly, Fight, and Win.*
> *I am faithful to a Proud Heritage,*
> *A Tradition of Honor,*
> *And a Legacy of Valor.*
>
> *I am an American Airman.*
> *Guardian of Freedom and Justice,*
> *My Nation's Sword and Shield,*
> *Its Sentry and Avenger.*
> *I defend my Country with my Life.*

RANK INSIGNIA OF THE U.S. ARMED FORCES

ENLISTED

	E-1	E-2	E-3	E-4	E-5	E-6	E-7	E-8	E-9	SENIOR ENLISTED ADVISORS

ARMY

E-1	E-2	E-3	E-4	E-5	E-6	E-7	E-8		E-9		SENIOR ENLISTED ADVISORS
no insignia	Private E-2 (PV2)	Private First Class (PFC)	Specialist (SPC) / Corporal (CPL)	Sergeant (SGT)	Staff Sergeant (SSG)	Sergeant First Class (SFC)	Master Sergeant (MSG)	First Sergeant (1SG)	Sergeant Major (SGM)	Command Sergeant Major (CSM)	Sergeant Major of the Army (SMA)
Private E-1 (PV1)											

MARINES

no insignia	Private First (PFC)	Lance Corporal (LCpl)	Corporal (Cpl)	Sergeant (Sgt)	Staff Sergeant (SSgt)	Gunnery Sergeant (GySgt)	Master Sergeant (MSgt) / First Sergeant (1stSgt)	Master Gunnery Sergeant (MGySgt)	Sergeant Major (SgtMaj)	Sergeant Major of the Marine Corps (SgtMajMC)
Private (Pvt)										

AIR FORCE

no insignia	Airman (Amn)	Airman First Class (A1C)	Senior Airman (SrA)	Staff Sergeant (SSgt)	Technical Sergeant (TSgt)	Master Sergeant (MSgt) / First Sergeant (E-7)	Senior Master Sergeant (SMSgt) / First Sergeant (E-8)	Chief Master Sergeant (CMSgt) / First Sergeant (E-9) / Command Chief Master Sergeant (CCM)	Chief Master Sergeant of the Air Force (CMSAF)
Airman Basic (AB)									

NAVY

no insignia	Seaman Apprentice (SA)	Seaman (SN)	Petty Officer Third Class (PO3)	Petty Officer Second Class (PO2)	Petty Officer First Class (PO1)	Chief Petty Officer (CPO)	Senior Chief Petty Officer (SCPO)	Master Chief Petty Officer (MCPO) / Force or Fleet Command Master Chief Petty Officer (FORMC) (FLTMC)	Master Chief Petty Officer of the Navy (MCPON)
Seaman Recruit (SR)									

COAST GUARD

no insignia	Seaman Apprentice (SA)	Seaman (SN)	Petty Officer Third Class (PO3)	Petty Officer Second Class (PO2)	Petty Officer First Class (PO1)	Chief Petty Officer (CPO)	Senior Chief Petty Officer (SCPO)	Master Chief Petty Officer (MCPO) / Command Master Chief (CMC)	Master Chief Petty Officer of the Coast Guard (MCPO-CG)
Seaman Recruit (SR)									

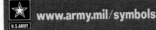

www.army.mil/symbols

RANK INSIGNIA OF THE U.S. ARMED FORCES

OFFICERS

O-1	O-2	O-3	O-4	O-5	O-6	O-7	O-8	O-9	O-10	SPECIAL

ARMY - AIR FORCE - MARINES

Second Lieutenant (2LT)	First Lieutenant (1LT)	Captain (CPT)	Major (MAJ)	Lieutenant Colonel (LTC)	Colonel (COL)	Brigadier General (BG)	Major General (MG)	Lieutenant General (LTG)	General (GEN)	General of the Army (GA)

NAVY - COAST GUARD

Ensign (ENS)	Lieutenant Junior Grade (LTJG)	Lieutenant (LT)	Lieutenant Commander (LCDR)	Commander (CDR)	Captain (CAPT)	Rear Admiral Lower Half (RADM)(L)	Rear Admiral Upper Half (RADM)(U)	Vice Admiral (VADM)	Admiral (ADM)	Fleet Admiral (FADM)

W-1	W-2	W-3	W-4	W-5

ARMY

Warrant Officer (WO1)	Chief Warrant Officer (CW2)	Chief Warrant Officer (CW3)	Chief Warrant Officer (CW4)	Chief Warrant Officer (CW5)

NAVY - COAST GUARD

Warrant Officer 1 W-1 * The grade of Warrant Officer W-1 is no longer in use.	Chief Warrant Officer (CWO2)	Chief Warrant Officer (CWO3)	Chief Warrant Officer (CWO4)	NO Chief Warrant Officer (CWO5)

MARINES

Warrant Officer (WO)	Chief Warrant Officer (CWO2)	Chief Warrant Officer (CWO3)	Chief Warrant Officer (CWO4)	Chief Warrant Officer (CWO5)

AIR FORCE

NO WARRANT	NO WARRANT	NO WARRANT	NO WARRANT	NO WARRANT

www.army.mil/symbols

U.S.ARMY

I am an American Airman.
Wingman, Leader, Warrior.
I will never leave an Airman behind,
I will never falter,
And I will not fail.

Information General to All Branches of the Military

General Orders of a Sentry. The general orders are what you do when you are standing guard. The Air Force has changed its rules slightly and you do not need to memorize the general orders. Instead, when you stand guard, you will have instructions in front of you that you are to follow. However, it is still a good idea to look over the general orders, so that you know the basics. The Coast Guard, Marine Corps, and Navy have eleven general orders, while the Army has a condensed, three-item list of orders. Here is the Army version, which is similar to what is used by the Air Force:

1. *I will guard everything within the limits of my post and quit my post only when properly relieved.*
   - You are in charge of the area assigned to you and must remain in charge until the next assigned guard arrives to take over from you.
2. *I will obey my special orders and perform all of my duties in a military manner.*
   - You must follow all instructions given to you when you took charge of your guard post and you must behave professional and responsibly while on duty.
3. *I will report violations of my special orders, emergencies, and anything not covered in my instructions to the commander of the relief.*
   - This means that you must tell your instructor about any and all problems that occur while you are on guard, such as if someone tries to enter without authorization.

Military Alphabet. The branches of the military have a shared phonetic alphabet. A phonetic alphabet is an alphabet where a sound or a word represents a letter. You know how when people spell something over the phone and the letters "b" and "v" or "t" and "p" sound very similar? That's why the military uses the phonetic alphabet instead. "Bravo" and "Victor" sound very different and keep personnel from getting letters confused when communicating. Here is the military phonetic alphabet:

Letter	Phonetic Word	Letter	Phonetic Word
A	Alpha	N	November
B	Bravo	O	Oscar
C	Charlie	P	Papa
D	Delta	Q	Quebec
E	Echo	R	Romeo
F	Foxtrot	S	Sierra
G	Golf	T	Tango
H	Hotel	U	Uniform
I	India	V	Victor
J	Juliet	W	Whiskey
K	Kilo	X	X-Ray
L	Lima (LEE-ma)	Y	Yankee
M	Mike	Z	Zulu

Military Time. Military time is designed to prevent confusion when information is communicated between personnel, just like the military alphabet. Military time is based on twenty-four hours rather than twelve. You do not have to use A.M. or P.M., because all of the hours are different. The word "zero" is used in every spot that doesn't have a number 1–9 and you do not use a colon between the hours and the minutes. So 2:05A.M. would be Zero two zero five or 0205.

Time	Military Time	Pronunciation
12 A.M.	0000	Zero-zero-zero-zero
1 A.M.	0100	Zero one hundred
2 A.M.	0200	Zero two hundred
3 A.M.	0300	Zero three hundred
4 A.M.	0400	Zero four hundred
5 A.M.	0500	Zero five hundred
6 A.M.	0600	Zero six hundred

7 A.M.	0700	Zero seven hundred
8 A.M.	0800	Zero eight hundred
9 A.M.	0900	Zero nine hundred
10 A.M.	1000	Ten hundred
11 A.M.	1100	Eleven hundred
12 P.M.	1200	Twelve hundred
1 P.M.	1300	Thirteen hundred
2 P.M.	1400	Fourteen hundred
3 P.M.	1500	Fifteen hundred
4 P.M.	1600	Sixteen hundred
5 P.M.	1700	Seventeen hundred
6 P.M.	1800	Eighteen hundred
7 P.M.	1900	Nineteen hundred
8 P.M.	2000	Twenty hundred
9 P.M.	2100	Twenty-one hundred
10 P.M.	2200	Twenty-two hundred
11 P.M.	2300	Twenty-three hundred

Military Terminology. As you can see, the military likes to use its own words and abbreviations. This can be confusing until you get used to it. Your training instructors will be more than happy to tell you what they want you to call things, but if you get a basic grasp of terms before you leave for training, you'll feel less like you wandered into foreign country. There is a glossary in the back that has basic terms used throughout this book and there are several sources of information online:

- The Department of Defense: *http://www.dtic.mil/doctrine/dod_dictionary*
- TodaysMilitary.com: *http://www.todaysmilitary.com/inside/military-glossary*
- Airmen Families: *https://airmenfamilies.com/main/recruiting-process/air-force-glossary*

Uniform Code of Military Justice. The Uniform Code of Military Justice (UCMJ) is the body of military law. Parts of it spell out what happens to military personnel when they break the law. While you do not need to memorize the UCMJ (it's too long for that), you should read it over. As soon as you take the final Oath of Enlistment and leave for basic training, you are bound by the UCMJ and can be court-martialed for infractions. The parts of the UCMJ can be found here: *http://www.law.cornell.edu/uscode/html/uscode10/usc_sup_01_10_10_A_20_II_30_47.html.*

Your Social Security Number. The Air Force will need you to fill out many forms, right when you first arrive at basic training, while you're still shell-shocked. Your Social Security number will need to be written on almost all of them, so it is important that you have it memorized before you arrive. It is also a good idea to know just the last four digits of your number as that is often used to identify you while you are in the military.

What You Don't Need to Learn in Advance

One aspect of preparing for recruit training might surprise you — you do not need to learn how to handle a weapon before you leave for training. The Air Force has a specific way they teach recruits to shoot and they've found that those recruits who enter basic training never having handled a weapon are much more likely to qualify on their first try and to earn marksmanship medals than those recruits who have grown up around guns. That's because recruits who have never fired a weapon don't have to unlearn poor habits, whereas the recruits who are more familiar with firearms don't always listen as carefully to instructions and then make mistakes.

The best way you can prepare for military weapons training is to relax and not worry about it. Your instructors will teach you everything you need to know and as long as you don't stress about it, you will do just fine. If you already know your way around a gun, then your best bet is to forget everything you have learned and go into Air Force training willing to start learning about weapons from the basics on up. Be open to learning the Air Force way to shoot and be eager to listen to everything your instructors tell you and you will qualify quickly.

You also do not have to learn how to drill, or march in formation, before you leave. Your instructors do not expect you to know how to drill when you arrive and they will begin showing you the basics as soon as you arrive. If you want to know more about military drill, however, it doesn't hurt to look over the basics of Air Force drill, so that you understand the general terms before you get to training. More information can be found here: *http://usmilitary.about.com/od/the orderlyroom/l/bldrill.htm.*

Social Preparation

In addition to preparing your mind and body for the basic training experience, you will need to make sure to put your bills and other affairs in order. That way problems will not arise while you are in training and unable to deal with them. Also, you will need to get your friends and family ready for you to be gone.

Getting Your Affairs in Order

There are things you will need to be sure to organize before you leave because you will not be able to take care of them while you are in basic training.

- *Open a bank or credit union account.* If you do not already have an account with a bank or a credit union, you will need to open one. Your recruiter can tell you what credit unions are common to Air Force bases, if you prefer to have an account at one of them. Otherwise, you can simply choose a bank that is convenient to you at this time. Be sure to get a debit card and to verify that it works before leaving for basic training.
- *Set up direct deposit.* Your recruiter will have the form for you to set up direct deposit of your military pay into your bank or credit union account. NOTE: Military pay can take 30 to 45 days to get started in direct deposit, so it is a good idea to have some money in your account in case of emergencies. One to two hundred dollars will work if you can afford it.
- *Bills.* You will not have access to your bank account, a computer,

a check card, etc. while you are in training. Here are some suggestions for handling bills for your house, car, etc.:

- *Pay off as many as possible.* If you leave for basic training debt free, then you won't have bills hanging over your head after graduation.
- *Arrange for automatic payments.* Any bills that you cannot pay off should be set up to be automatically paid from your bank or credit union account.
- *Have a trustworthy person handle them.* If you are married, this will be your spouse. Otherwise, choose someone who is financially responsible. A drinking buddy or someone you are dating is not a good choice.

- *Car.* If your car or other vehicle is paid off, does not have great sentimental value to you, and is not needed by your family, then you might consider selling it so that you don't have to worry about it while you're gone. Otherwise, arrange for the payment to be made automatically. If you leave it with someone, make sure they are trustworthy and that either your or their insurance will allow them to drive it if that is okay with you. Or you can arrange for it to be kept in storage until after graduation. If your driver's license or vehicle registration will expire while you are gone, see if you can go ahead and renew them before you leave.
- *Cellphone.* As of February 2012, the Air Force is the only branch of the military that allows recruits to bring their cellphones to basic training with them. Your training instructor will keep it while you are in training and give it back to you when you are allowed to make phone calls. Check with your cellphone company to see if you can pay your bill in advance so that you do not have to worry about it while you are in training. Otherwise, set up direct payment as you do with your other bills.
- *Paperwork.* Make sure you have copies of the documents you may need at basic training. These could include your marriage license, divorce paperwork, Social Security card, etc. While

you're gone, important papers should be stored in a fireproof safe and the key should be given to a trustworthy family member or friend. If you are married, make sure that you give your spouse power of attorney which will allow them to sign in your name while you are away. Your recruiter can help you get the correct form and fill it out.

- *Legal issues.* You will not be able to leave for basic training with outstanding legal issues. Resolve any legal problems as quickly as possible and avoid getting involved in any new issues, even minor ones such as traffic violations. Keep your recruiter apprised of any legal problems you encounter during the DEP.

GETTING YOUR FAMILY AND FRIENDS READY FOR YOUR ABSENCE

Leaving family and friends for nine weeks is hard for you, but it will also be hard on them. You can help ease their pain before you leave and they can help support you while you're gone.

- *Encourage them to write to you.* During Air Force recruit training you will only occasionally be allowed to make brief phone calls, so mail is very important way for you to stay in contact with your friends and family. You can get mail every day except Sundays and holidays. You will be given time to write home, so ask your friends and family to write to you.

  Letters from home should be upbeat and cheerful. Ask them to help you keep your spirits up by offering words of encouragement. Bad news is sometimes unavoidable, but it helps if family and friends use their letters to you to relay mostly good things that happen. Even simple details of home life can help. They are welcome to send pictures, but care packages are not allowed.

  To help ensure you receive letters, partially address and stamp envelopes to yourself before you leave. You'll find out the rest of the needed information for your address once you get to training and you'll have the opportunity to send it to your friends and family so that they can write to you. Your address will be:

> AB [Airman Basic] [Your last name, your first name, your middle initial]
> [Your training squadron #] TRS/ FLT [your flight #]/ Dorm [your dorm #]
> [Your dorm's street address]. Unit [your unit #]
> Lackland AFB, TX 78236 — [zip code extension]

- *Help your children understand what you'll be doing.* If you are a parent, then you'll need to prepare your kids for your absence. There are books for younger readers about the Air Force in the "For More Information" section. Reading these with your child will help him or her understand your new job. You can also watch some of the videos about recruit training listed in that section, so that they can see what you'll be experiencing. Ask your kids to write to you every day and promise that you'll write to them as well.
- *Have a going away party.* This is a great way to enjoy time with friends and family, but there are a few things to keep in mind.
    - *Don't have the party the night before you leave.* You'll want to be rested, not tired from staying up all night. Instead have your get-together the weekend before you leave.
    - *Don't use drugs at the party, do not have unprotected sex, and do not drink if you are underage.* Drugs and alcohol in your system will be discovered upon your arrival at basic training and unprotected sex could lead to pregnancy or a disease. All of these will keep you from completing training.
- *Remind them that you love them and that their support is important to your success.* They probably know it, but it's nice to hear again.

156

Emotional Preparation

Even if you are entering basic training dreaming of becoming a hardened warrior, you will still want to prepare yourself emotionally for the adventure on which you are about to embark. Begin by psyching yourself up during your time in the DEP.

- *Don't go in thinking that training will be too difficult.* You've prepared yourself during your time in the DEP, so you are ready for recruit training.
- *Enter basic training eager to learn.* Recruit training is all about learning the basics of being an Airman. By the time you leave for training, you should be excited about spending all day every day learning something new. That excitement will carry you through any rough patches.
- *Know that training is planned so as to give you the tools you need.* Every lesson you will learn in recruit training will prepare you for the next lesson. Pay attention and work hard and you *will* learn what you need to learn.
- *Remember that recruit training is not what life in the Air Force will be like every day.* Recruit training is only nine weeks long. You *can* get through it and then you will go on to enjoy being an Airman.
- *Believe that you can succeed.* The Air Force selected you just as much as you selected them. They saw something in you; now you need to see it in yourself. If you want to be an Airman and you work with that goal in mind, then you will succeed.

If you want to give yourself a lift while you are at recruit training, sit down and write yourself nine letters or postcards. In each one, remind yourself why you decided to become an Airman, tell yourself that you are determined to succeed, and offer yourself encouraging words. You can slip in a photograph of a pet or your family or your friends; something that will make you smile when you see it. Stamp the letters or postcards and put a date on the outside of each one — one letter or postcard per week of basic training. Then give the letters to your recruiter, a parent, or a trusted friend and ask them to mail one to you each week while you are at basic training.

As your time in the DEP is drawing to a close, start looking towards the future. Soon you will leave for basic training and your journey to becoming an Airman will begin. To give you an idea of what to expect during those nine weeks, the next chapter will tell you what happens in basic training, from the moment you arrive until the day you proudly graduate.

FOUR

Air Force
Basic Training

Overview

The goal of basic training, also called recruit training, is to take a civilian and turn him or her into a basic Airman. Basic training is just that — the *basic* knowledge that new military members need to become a part of the Air Force. Recruits learn how to march, how to use a variety of weapons, how to fight, how to maneuver in a variety of conditions, how to administer first aid, how to read standard navigational aids, how to work as part of a team, as well as learning military and Air Force history, ethics, etiquette, customs, dress, etc.

Air Force basic training lasts for eight weeks. Before basic training begins, new recruits go through half a week of reception, called Zero Week, so they are at their training location for eight and a half weeks overall. Every day of the week is a training day, even Sundays and even holidays, though recruits are allowed time for religious activities on Sunday mornings (more information on religious services is in Chapter 20). Recruits spend their days doing physical training, learning military skills (either in the classroom or hands on), and practicing what they've been taught. Training personnel make sure that even mundane activities like cleaning the barracks (called "dorms" in the Air Force) are an opportunity for learning how to do things the military and Air Force way.

Air Force Basic Training Location

The Air Force trains recruits at Lackland Air Force Base in San Antonio, Texas. Recruits have been training at Lackland since 1946. The weather in San Antonio is generally mild, though it can still be chilly on winter mornings and it will definitely be hot in the summer. Currently 35,000 recruits a year train at Lackland, divided into seven training squadrons, each of which is further divided into roughly ten flights of 45 to 60 recruits each. There are two support squadrons. The 737th Training Support Squadron oversees the reception of new recruits and also handles graduation activities. The 319th Training Support Squadron oversees, trains, and rehabilitates recruits who are injured, as well as those who are being removed from the Air Force.

Military Training Instructors

Military training instructors — commonly called training instructors or TIs — are the main training personnel in charge of recruits. Usually each flight of recruits has one or two TIs. The TIs oversee all aspects of their flight's training, acting as a father or mother figure to the

Military training instructors are easily identified by their "Smokey the Bear" hat and their in-your-face teaching (Official U.S. Air Force photograph by Senior Airman Christopher Griffin).

recruits, motivating them or challenging them, or acting as a disciplinarian, correcting behavioral problems. TIs are responsible for teaching their recruits all of the knowledge required to graduate from basic military training, from how to drill (or march in formation), to how to maintain their gear, to how to act in a military manner, and more.

Training instructors are highly trained individuals. They are senior enlisted personnel who must complete a course that recreates every aspect of basic training. During their training, they learn how to motivate, instruct, and discipline. They must memorize all possible drill routines and be completely familiar with the standard operating procedures that training instructors must follow.

Airmen serve as training instructors for four years and while they are in charge of a training flight they can work upwards of 120 hours a week, on very little sleep and without seeing their families. They know how to do, and have done, everything that they tell recruits to do. Training instructors are the only Airmen who wear the distinctive campaign hat — aka, the "Smokey the Bear" hat.

Gender Integrated Training

The Air Force trains male and female recruits side-by-side in what are called brother/sister flights, meaning two flights — one male and one female — that train together, but are housed separately. The TIs of the brother/sister flights work together to plan and organize training. (The Marine Corps is the only branch of the service that trains men and women completely separately.) Training for males and females is exactly the same, though a few of the female physical requirements are lighter. Because there are more male training instructors than there are female ones, it is likely that a female flight will have a male TI. Male TIs have strict rules about when they can and cannot enter the dorms of female flights and there are procedures for how they must announce themselves when they do so. Not all brother flights have a sister flight.

Since there are more men training than women, most flight pairs will be brother/brother.

Training Schedule

The first three days at basic training are called Zero Week. During this time new recruits receive their gear and undergo a series of medical and physical fitness tests to make sure they are ready for basic training. On the Friday of Zero Week, the training squadron officially starts basic military training.

Air Force recruit training is divided into three phases. The three phases are designed to train recruits how to prepare for a wartime deployment, function during a deployment, and complete the tasks necessary after a deployment is finished.

- *Deployment Preparation*: Weeks One through Five. During this time recruits learn the basic military skills and the warrior skills needed to operate during a wartime deployment.
- *Deployment, called Basic Expeditionary Airman Skills Training, aka "BEAST"*: Week Six. During this time recruits run a deployment scenario, putting into practice the skills learned during Deployment Preparation.
- *Reconstitution Time*: Weeks Seven and Eight. During this time recruits complete the tasks that follow a deployment and they learn the basic Airmanship skills which will be used when they move out into the regular Air Force. Reconstitution Time ends with Graduation.

After graduation, new Airmen usually get a day off to spend with their family and then they leave for job training.

Basic Training Tips

Air Force basic training is designed to break down you as a civilian and remake you into an Airman. But this process cannot happen without your help. That means that in order to succeed in basic training you have to *decide* that you are going to succeed. There are things you can do that will help ensure you have a successful time in basic training.

- *Adjust your attitude.* You might be the best student in your school or the toughest person in your neighborhood, but the moment you set foot on Lackland Air Force Base you become the lowest rung of the ladder. You are not known by any title except trainee until you show — by successfully graduating — that you have earned the right to a rank and to be called an Airman. High and mighty attitudes and chips on your shoulder have no place in recruit training, not with your training instructors and not with your fellow recruits.
- *Accept the loss of freedom.* You will have to do what the military says; there is no way to get around that. Fighting the system will only frustrate you. Instead accept that you are giving up some freedoms and remind yourself of what you are receiving in return. After all, even if you stayed a civilian and got a job in an office or a factory or a store, you would still have to bend to the rules of your organization.
- *Don't take things personally.* Training instructors are going to yell, but they don't do it because they hate you. They do this to see how you handle yourself when you are under stress. Combat is stressful and the Air Force needs personnel who can keep going

even when tired and harassed. Know that the yelling and the other stresses are not directed at you personally and know that learning to handle them will make you a stronger person.

- *Don't be lazy and don't give up.* Training instructors want recruits who work hard, try their best, and don't quit. Nothing will make them mad faster than laziness or recruits who stop before giving everything they can. If they think you can keep going, then you can. Ignore the voice in your head telling you to stop. Persevere. You'll be surprised by how much you can accomplish.

- *Don't show off.* Just as you don't want to give up too soon, you also don't want to always strive to beat everyone around you. That is not the sign of a good leader or a good teammate and the Air Force wants recruits who can be both. The only person you are competing with is yourself. Be the best *you* can be at everything you are assigned and don't worry about trying to outdo your fellow recruits. Basic training is about what *you* can accomplish. Those recruits who excel and win awards are the ones who aren't trying for acclaim. They are simply doing their very best every single day of training.

- *Do what you are told, when you are told, and how you are told— without question.* In a combat situation there is not time to question orders. Your training instructors are preparing you for that now by expecting you to immediately obey every order — no matter how bizarre or impossible — without questioning. The sooner you learn to do this, the easier time you'll have during recruit training.

- *Tell the truth and do not make excuses.* NEVER lie to your training instructors for any reason. They will know that you lied and they will make your life harder because of it. If you made a mistake, admit to it, but don't try to explain why. If you don't know the answer, admit to it. Your life will be much easier if you keep things honest and if you don't try to justify your actions.

- *Pay close attention. Pay especially close attention to safety issues.* No matter how tired you are, pay attention to everything your training instructors say. Often they will be giving you hints (or even outright telling you) about what you can expect during training or the best way to complete an exercise. Pay even closer attention when they are talking about safety. The military takes safety very seriously, especially during training. Nothing will get you in trouble faster than ignoring or forgetting instructions.

- *Encourage teamwork.* Teamwork is paramount to military life. The Air Force will expect you to immediately work as a team with your fellow recruits. Your training instructors will not care if you don't like someone. In fact, not liking them makes it even more likely that you will be forced to work together! The faster you and your fellow recruits learn to work together — in the field, in the dorms, and in the classroom — the better your basic training experience will be.

- *Look out for your fellow Airmen.* Part of the Airman Creed is "I will never leave an Airman behind." This philosophy begins in basic training. Whenever possible, help out your fellow recruits and they, in turn, will help you.

- *Deal with differences maturely.* Your fellow recruits will be from all parts of the country, all types of backgrounds, all ages, all levels of education, and all political and religious beliefs. It is your responsibility to be respectful of those differences. That doesn't mean you have to like all of your fellow recruits and it doesn't mean you can resort to violence to "get them in line"; it means you have to find a way to interact like mature adults. Focus on the mission at hand and you will soon find that differences don't matter as much as teamwork.

- *Be the type of leader you would want to follow.* The Air Force wants its Airmen to be leaders, but being a leader doesn't mean that you are bossy or mean or that you look down on those below you. Think about the kind of leader you respect. What does he or she do that makes them a good leader? That is the type of person you should strive to be when you are placed in a leadership role, both during basic training and after.

- *Take every opportunity to learn from those around you.* You will be amazing how much you will learn just from watching your fellow recruits, your training instructors, and the other personnel you encounter. Go into basic training believing that every person you meet will teach you something and be eager to accept those lessons.

- *Make friends.* You are training with the people who could one day stand beside you in combat. Get to know them, ask about their background and interests and reasons for enlisting, find out who they are. Having friends will make your time in basic training a shared experience rather than a solo survival expedition.

- *Take care of your body.* Injuries and illnesses will, at best, make training harder. At the worst, they could cause you to be set back in training or even put an end to training all together. Drink plenty of water. Keep your nails clipped, powder your feet, and tend to blisters. Wash your hands regularly, especially before eating or after going to the bathroom. If you hurt yourself or think you are sick, tell your training instructor immediately, no matter how fearsome he or she is. Training instructors are trained both to spot fakers and to see the signs of serious injury or illness, so he or she will know if you are well enough to continue training or if you need to visit a doctor.

- *Use "free time" to your advantage.* You won't get a lot of time to yourself, but you will get some and that time can help you recharge and regroup. Use free time to study, write letters to friends and family, and get to know your fellow recruits.

- *Develop a military bearing.* No matter what the situation, no matter how much you are being yelled at, no matter whose fault a problem is, you need to remain calm, collected, and mature. Don't whine, try to explain, or display emotions. If you act like you are calm and rational, then you will soon be calm and rational, even when you are faced with combat stresses. Learn to let distractions — such as training instructors in your face — roll off your back.

- *Ask for help if you need it.* If you are injured, sick, or if you begin to have suicidal thoughts, you must ask for help immediately. Do not allow fear of your training instructor or of getting set back to keep you from getting the help you need. It is more important that you treat the problem up front, before it becomes a much bigger issue. Likewise, if you are having trouble understanding some aspect of training, ask your fellow trainees to help you study. They are likely to appreciate the chance to help you, especially since it means they'll be getting in valuable studying at the same time.
- *Remember that basic training is NOT what life in the military is like.* The goal of Air Force recruit training is to turn you from a civilian into an Airman. Your training instructors do this by breaking you down and then rebuilding you. After you graduate successfully from basic training, you will still have to work hard and remain professional, but you will not be faced with the same deprivations and strictures that you must live with during basic training.
- *Keep a positive attitude.* This can be hard, especially when you are feeling frustrated, tired, sore, discouraged, and/or homesick, but you have to stay positive. Think of each day as a new chance to try your hardest. Focus on the short term goal of getting through one day at a time and don't forget the long term goal or goals that led you to join the Air Force. Remember that thousands of men and women have gone through basic training successfully and you can too. At the end of each day, remind yourself of at least one good thing you accomplished that day and begin to look forward to the next day as another opportunity to learn. Each day is one day closer to you becoming an Airman!

Leaving for
Basic Training

During the weeks you've spent in the Delayed Entry Program, you've been working hard to get ready to leave for basic training. You should now be excited and eager and, most of all, ready to begin your new journey.

Final Preparations

As the time draws closer for you to leave for basic training, your recruiter will meet with you to go over your paperwork again. Make sure that everything is correct. Once you get to basic training, you will not be able to make changes. If something is not in your enlistment contract — whether it be a promotion, a job, or something else — then it doesn't exist. Read your contract carefully and make sure changes are made as soon as needed.

You will go back to the Military Entrance Processing Station (MEPS) to complete your paperwork, get reexamined by the doctors to make sure any medical issues have not arisen since your last visit, and to take the final Oath of Enlistment. Your recruiter will also make sure that nothing has happened to change your eligibility. During your time in the Delayed Entry Program you should have been keeping your recruiter apprised of any problems or changes that might affect your eligibility. It is better to address such issues now rather than wait until basic training. Once you take the final Oath of Enlistment and ship to basic training, you are bound by the Uniform Code of

Military Justice and are subject to court-martial if you break military law.

After your recruiter has gone over your paperwork and after the doctors have looked you over again, then you will be discharged from the Delayed Entry Program. You then take the Oath of Enlistment for the second and final time. (If you are enlisting as a reservist, then you will not need to take the Oath again. You became a part of the military as soon as you took the Oath the first time.) As mentioned in Chapter 12: Visiting the Military Entrance Processing Station (MEPS), the Oath of Enlistment is a serious, solemn vow. You should not take it lightly. Read over it once more and make sure you are able to agree to it, freely and clearly.

> *I, _____, do solemnly swear (or affirm) that I will support and defend the Constitution of the United States against all enemies, foreign and domestic; that I will bear true faith and allegiance to the same; and that I will obey the orders of the President of the United States and the orders of the officers appointed over me, according to regulations and the Uniform Code of Military Justice. So help me God.*

Family members are welcome to attend your swearing of the Oath. After the ceremony is over, you should say good-bye to them, because you'll be leaving for basic training and they will not be able to go with you past this point.

Your travel to basic training will be arranged for you. Your recruiter will make sure that you know where you need to go and how you are getting there, whether you are traveling by bus or plane and whether or not you need to spend the night anywhere. All of your travel to basic training is paid for, as are any meals or hotel visits.

Packing for the Journey

Each branch of the military will give you a list of what to bring with you to basic training. You should bring with you ONLY:

- *Needed documents*: your Social Security Card, your driver's license or picture ID, your permanent resident alien/green card (if applicable), and any other paperwork or documents your recruiter gives you or tells you to bring (such as your marriage certificate, your child/children's birth certificate(s), etc.)

- *Prescription medicines*: also bring a paper copy of the prescription from your doctor; this is assuming that the medicines have already been approved by the doctors at MEPS
- *Duffel bag or small suitcase*: do not bring an overly large bag; pick the smallest bag possible to fit the items you are bringing and only bring what you absolutely need
- *Eyeglasses and contact lenses*: bring both even if you normally only wear contacts
- *Twenty dollars in cash*
- *Your recruiter's business card*
- *Religious material*: a necklace and/or a religious book (if applicable)
- *Photos*: wallet-sized only; nothing pornographic
- *Notebook and a ballpoint pen*
- *Laundry soap/detergent*: enough for one or two loads
- *Toiletries*
  - All recruits should bring:
    - *Soap*: one bar of soap in a travel case
    - *Toothbrush and toothpaste*: toothbrush should be in a case
    - *Deodorant*: non-aerosol
    - *Shampoo*
  - Male recruits should bring:
    - *Razor, shaving cream, shaving kit*
  - Female recruits can bring if desired:
    - *Hair care accessories*: brush and/or comb, plus elastics, bobby pins, etc. that match your hair color
    - *Razor, shaving cream or gel*
    - *Feminine hygiene items*: If it is your time of the month, you can bring supplies with you, but you do not need

to bring enough for all of basic training, as you will
have the opportunity to purchase more once you are
issued supplies.

- *Clothing*
  - All recruits should bring:
    - *Civilian clothing*: enough for three days, but do not
      pack an excessive amount; make sure they are neat and
      clean and weather appropriate (no shorts in the winter),
      but that you are able to move in them
    - *Shower shoes*: flip-flops/thong sandals; plain and simple
      is best
  - Female recruits should also bring:
    - *Underwear*: six pairs of white or neutral cotton under-
      pants; no thongs
    - *Bras*: six white or neutral bras; these can be regular or
      sports bras or a mix of both; be sure they are supportive
      enough for activity
    - *Nylons/pantyhose*: flesh-toned; will be worn with dress
      uniform at the end of training
    - *Spandex shorts*: these are optional; they are worn beneath
      your workout gear; shorts should be black and not too
      short in the legs
- *Optional items:* Recruits may bring, if they choose:
  - *Supplies for letter writing*: 1 box of envelopes; small address
    book with your family and friends' contact information; 1
    book of stamps; other stationery supplies
  - *Laundry care items*: an iron; spray starch (non-aerosol); a
    sewing kit
  - *Additional hygiene items*: 1 box of cotton balls; nail trimmers/
    clippers; foot powder; two towels
  - *Two D batteries*
  - *Watch*: one that is waterproof, non-descript, and has a sec-
    ond hand is best
  - *Running shoes and socks:* you can buy running shoes during

Zero Week, but if you have a pair that works well for you, bring them; they should not be too brightly or garishly colored or decorated; you can also bring three pairs of white running socks

o *Cellphone or calling cards*: you may bring your cell phone, but it will be kept in your training instructor's office; remove any pornographic or explicit content on the phone before leaving for basic training; if you do not have a cell phone, you may bring calling cards so that you can make phone calls home

You should not bring any weapons, playing cards, dice, pornography, food, gum, tobacco products, alcohol, illegal drugs, over-the-counter drugs (not even aspirin), jewelry (except for a wedding ring and/or a religious necklace), electronic devices (such as MP3 players or video game consoles), cameras, make-up, nail polish, large amounts of money, or any valuables. BE SURE to turn your cellphone off as soon as you get on the bus to travel to the recruit training depot. You can bring a book or magazine with you if you need something to keep you occupied during your travels, but leave it at the airport or bus station for future passengers to enjoy. Since you don't need to bring much with you, leave large bags and purses at home. Bring a bag small enough to carry just your needed supplies.

Please note that your recruiter will give you the latest list of what you can and cannot bring with you to basic training. Follow that list exactly. It will save you a lot of hassle and insure that you are not singled out by the training instructors when you first get to training.

You'll want to wear comfortable clothes for your journey, but make sure they look neat and professional. Khaki slacks with a polo or long sleeve shirt are good choices. Try to wear pants with pockets because you'll need a place to hold a pen and other items once you get to the reception area. Roll down your sleeves, tuck in your shirt, and button your top collar button as soon as you get on the bus to the recruit training depot. You will be on your feet a lot, so wear shoes that support your feet. Closed-toe shoes with socks are best. Do not wear any earrings or nail polish. You do not want to stand out in any way when you arrive because that will guarantee that you will be harassed by instructors. Instead, aim to look bland and professional.

Men do not need to get a haircut before leaving for basic training (your head will be shaved soon enough!), but you should make sure your hair looks tidy. Women do not need to get their hair cut before training, even though they won't be getting their head shaved. But during training you'll need to keep your hair up and off your collar, so a shorter, easy to manage cut is a good idea. Before arriving at training, female recruits should put their hair into a bun or other neat hairstyle that keeps the hair off of their collar.

During Your Travels

Depending on where you are coming from, you may travel by van, bus, or airplane in order to get to basic training. Your recruiter will make sure you have all of the information and tickets you need to get to where you are going. If you live close enough where you do not have to fly, then you probably won't need a meal voucher. (Sometimes, though, kindly bus drivers will stop to allow new recruits to get one last fast food meal before they get to training.)

If you are coming from farther away, then you'll fly into the nearest large airport to your recruit training depot and then take a bus or van from there. More than likely you'll get a meal voucher to spend at the airport. Be sure to throw away any leftover snacks or drinks before you get to basic training. You aren't allowed to bring them with you to basic training.

You may be the only person from your town or region heading to boot camp, but you'll meet up with other recruits soon enough. These are the men and women you'll be training alongside, so be friendly and approachable. If there is a group of recruits traveling together, MEPS or your recruiter will appoint one recruit as a leader of the small group.

It is the leader's job to make sure everyone gets to where they are sup-posed to be, when they are supposed to be there. The leader is also in charge of the group's official paperwork and must keep control of that paperwork at all times.

If you get separated from the group when traveling by air or if you run into any other problems, ask airport personnel to direct you to the nearest USO (United Service Organizations) office. There is usually a USO office in every airport and the personnel there can get you back on track. Otherwise, call your recruiter and explain the situation to him or her.

The United States Military Entrance Processing Command — the department that oversees all MEPS locations — has a video which explains recruit travel to basic training. It is particularly useful if you have never flown before, as it outlines all of the procedures for navigating through an airport. You can watch the video here: *http://www.mepcom. army.mil/travel-video.html.*

As mentioned before, you can bring a book or magazine to read while you are traveling and you should try to meet some of the other new recruits with whom you're traveling. But the most important thing you can do during your travels from home to recruit training is to rest. The days during Zero Week are long and sleepless and overwhelming. You will want to get as much rest beforehand as you can. All too soon your bus will be pulling into Lackland and your civilian life will end as your new military life begins.

Zero Week

Though you may hear that Air Force basic training is eight weeks long, it is actually closer to nine. The first three days are called Zero Week. That is the time when you are processed into the Air Force. While there you will fill out paperwork, get medical checkups, receive your gear, take your initial physical fitness test, and be added to your flight. While you are undergoing all of that work, your training instructor will be learning personal information about each of you, finishing up administrative details, transferring you to your new dorm, etc.

Zero Week can in many ways be more stressful than the rest of basic training. You are confused, tired, homesick, and, most of all, afraid you have made a terrible mistake. To make it worse, there is a lot of "hurry up and wait," so you have time to worry about what you've gotten yourself into. But don't let yourself get down. Focus on how each part of the receiving and forming process brings you one step closer to being an Airman. Now is not the time to decide you do not want to go through basic training. You are here and you must continue. Failure to train will only land you in the brig (jail) for disobeying orders.

Arriving at Basic Training

The 737th Training Support Squadron, which oversees Zero Week, must be highly organized in order to process the high number of recruits who arrive on Tuesday almost every week. Throughout the day they will get calls from the Air Force training instructors who are escorting recruits at the airport and other transportation stations with a head count, so that they know in advance how many recruits are arriving, when they will arrive, and their gender breakdown. When the bus carrying the new recruits passes through the gates at Lackland, the personnel at the gate call so that the training instructors at the welcome center can be ready to get things started.

You will likely arrive at the recruit training base at night, usually sometime between 8 P.M. and 2 A.M. When you arrive depends upon where you are traveling from and whether or not you have to wait for other recruits to join you. You might be on a bus filled with recruits or you could be in a passenger van with just a few other people. Either way, you will head into the welcome center and spend several hours filling out paperwork. The paperwork is important and will insure that you are properly processed, but — as with many things in basic training — it is also a way for the Air Force to get you used to following orders. One vital piece of information will be your squadron number and flight number. You should memorize them as soon as you are told

Training begins the moment you step off the bus at Lackland AFB (Official U.S. Air Force photograph; Training Development Flight).

them. Your job during those hours is to listen, closely and carefully. There may be some yelling and there will definitely be a lot of information thrown your way, but if you pay attention and don't panic, then you will get through without too much trouble.

The First Night of Zero Week

During your first night you will also have the opportunity to call home. If you have a cellphone with you, then you will use that; otherwise you will use a calling card and a phone will be provided for you. You will not have time for a leisurely chat. Instead you will be given a card with a scripted statement you must read. The statement will tell your family that you have arrived and that you will contact them soon, but that is about all you will be allowed to say. (Note: it is a good idea to prepare your family in advance for this call. Tell them that you will likely sound tired and nervous, but ask them to sound supportive and cheerful when they pick up. If they are distressed, then you will be worried about them at a time when you need to be focusing on yourself. Remind them that no matter how stressed you sound, you will be fine and you will adapt.)

After you have filled out your paperwork and made your phone call home, you will head to your dorm. Unlike all of the other branches of the military, where you do not meet the instructors who will be training you until after the reception period is over, in the Air Force you meet your training instructor (or instructors) right away. When you arrive at your dorm, your training instructor (TI) will be waiting for you. He or she will likely start the process of "shocking" you into obedience right away with a good amount of yelling and a lot of instructions, many of which may be confusing. Keep your cool as much as possible and try to do what you are told to the best of your ability. Soon your TI will allow you to head to bed for a few hours of sleep before waking you up and heading you back over to the welcome center for more processing.

The Rest of Zero Week

The first full day of Zero Week you will begin receiving your gear. There is a lot of gear given to you during basic training and you are expected to account for it. Some of your gear is yours permanently and you are charged for it. The charges come directly out of your paycheck, so you don't need to have money with you. Other gear is only yours temporarily while you are training and you will have to return it. You will be issued everything from uniforms (including outerwear, underwear, socks, shoes, hats, and belts) to school supplies (a guidebook of essential information) to hygiene items to military supplies (packs, canteens, rifles, rifle cleaning supplies, etc.), to miscellaneous items like combination locks. You will not receive your first uniform until the second or third day of Zero Week. Until then you will wear your civilian clothes.

The infamous haircuts are given during Zero Week. All male recruits will have their heads shaved. This is done quickly by a team of civilian barbers and soon all the male recruits have the same hairstyle. Female recruits do not have their hair cut. They should arrive at the recruit training facility with their hair already neat and up off of their collar.

Once you receive your gear and your uniform, you will turn in your personal effects, meaning the civilian clothes you arrived in. All of these items will be returned to you after training. You should not have brought much with you. (See Chapter 18 for a list of items to bring.) There will be a "Moment of Truth" where you can turn in any contraband, such as weapons, pornography, prescription drugs, etc. The Moment of Truth also allows you to confess to anything that you might not have told your recruiter about, such as a medical ailment like asthma or a minor criminal conviction. Ideally you will not have anything to report, since you will not have lied to your recruiter or omitted information. Lying during the Moment of Truth will not work as a way of getting out of basic training. The Air Force will be verifying anything you tell them and if they find that there is nothing preventing you from beginning training, then you *will* be beginning training. If

All male trainees will have their heads shaved when they arrive at recruit training (Official U.S. Air Force photograph; Training Development Flight).

your information is double-checked and it shows that you are ineligible for training, then you will be sent to the 319th Training Squadron to await processing to be sent back home.

Medical Testing and the Initial Physical Fitness Test

Much of the rest of Zero Week is taken up with medical testing. The doctors at basic training will put you through the same tests and evaluations that you underwent at MEPS. This is to ensure that any issues are caught before you begin training. It is important to remember that the doctors and nurses are not trying to disqualify you on purpose. They are only thinking of the greater good. What can be a simple problem for a civilian can be a major one for someone undergoing the rigors of military training. The medical personnel not only have to consider your safety and health, they have to consider how your physical issues will affect the units with which you will serve.

You will be drug tested again, so it should go without saying that you will not have been using any illegal drugs at any time before arriving at basic training. Female recruits will be tested for pregnancy and all recruits will be tested for sexually transmitted diseases. Additionally, you will visit the dentist who will evaluate your teeth and do any needed dental work. You will also visit an eye doctor who will check your eyes, verify your prescription (if you wear glasses or contacts), and issue you new, military-style glasses.

If major problems are found during your medical exams — problems which will prevent you from continuing training — you will be sent to the 319th Training Squadron to be processed out of the Air Force. Unfortunately that is the end of your military career, unless the issue is a temporary one which will clear up in a matter of months. From the 319th Training Squadron, you will be sent home.

You will take your initial physical fitness test during Zero Week. You must pass the this initial test to continue on to basic training. Here are the goals you must meet in order to pass:

Event	Initial PFT Minimum — Men
Run	1.5 mile run in 18 min. 30 sec.
Push-ups (in 2 min.)	5
Sit-ups (in 2 min.)	10

Event	Initial PFT Minimum — Women
Run	1.5 mile run in 21 min. 35 sec.
Push-ups (in 2 min.)	3
Sit-ups (in 2 min.)	5

Military Skills

In addition to filling out paperwork, getting gear issued to you, and undergoing medical evaluations, during Zero Week you will learn how to make up your bed in military fashion, learn how to address training instructors, and learn some basics of how to march. You will probably stand guard during the night and you will start getting used to following directions quickly and correctly.

During this time, your training instructors will learn about their new flight. They need to know who is left-handed, who is a reservist, what religions are represented, etc. They will make sure that you have all of your gear and that all your paperwork has been filled out and added to your file. They will get the flight settled into the dorm and make sure that you know how to store your gear, make up your rack, and do what you're told to do. By Friday your flight will be finished with Zero Week and ready to begin full basic training.

Life During Basic Training

The schedule for what happens when during basic training only tells part of the story. You're probably still wondering about the basic, day-to-day aspects of boot camp life. No one can completely prepare you for what you'll experience during basic training, because every recruit's time at boot camp is different, but the general details remain the same for all enlistees.

Addressing Your Training Instructors

Every branch of the service has a different way that military training instructors should be addressed. In the Air Force, you should always address your training instructor as "Training Instructor [Rank] [Name]." Your training instructors will expect you to answer using "sir" and "ma'am," but you don't need to use them at both the beginning and the end of your sentences, unlike some services. Just adding "sir" or "ma'am" to either the beginning or the end of your sentence will be fine. You will be taught the proper reporting statement to use: "Sir [or ma'am], trainee [your last name] reporting [or reports] as ordered." This sentence will be used before you respond to any questions.

Discipline and Punishment

Many people assume that training instructors can curse at, hit, bully, and abuse their recruits, but that is no longer the case. That does not mean, however, that training instructors have become gentle teddy bears. They are still allowed to "motivate" you, using a combination of yelling and physical exercise. Training instructors are taught how to motivate using a loud, powerful voice. You will quickly learn to listen to everything they are saying, because you want to be able to do what they want when they want it.

One unique aspect of the Air Force is the use of 341s. These are like demerit forms. You will be required to carry some of them with you at all times. Any time you violate the standards you should be upholding, the instructor who saw the infraction will have you hand over a 341. He or she will fill out the 341 with the details and the 341 will be given to your training instructor who will make the decision about appropriate punishments.

If you don't do what you are supposed to, then you'll most likely be disciplined using physical fitness drills. These drills are a series of exercises which are designed to get you in shape while also making you regret messing up. All exercises are carefully regulated and the training instructors have clear guidelines for using them.

Other acceptable punishments include removing your free time or assigning you to stand guard (waking up for an hour to keep watch while the other recruits sleep). You *will* experience some form of discipline during your time in recruit training, whether it is because you did something wrong or because your whole flight messed up or because one person messed up and your training instructor decided to make a point by punishing everyone. Whichever it is, know that it is coming and take it like an Airman.

Food and Sleep

You'll be so active during basic training that food and sleep may be two of your major concerns. Recruits are guaranteed seven to eight full hours of sleep a night — with a few exceptions. When you are standing guard or keeping watch, your sleep time may be cut down to six hours. During the BEAST, which is designed to see how you perform when overtired and stressed, you will get a lot less sleep per night.

The BEAST also changes your meals to two MREs (Meals Ready to Eat) and one hot meal per day. But during the rest of training you'll get three hot meals per day, eaten in the dining facility, where you'll have a choice of foods and drinks. You aren't given much time to eat — about 20 minutes — and you are not allowed to talk during the meal. Eat a balanced meal of proteins, vegetables, and carbohydrates, because you'll need the energy. Try to avoid sweets which will not stick with you between meals. During the summer months, you'll want to add extra salt to your food to replace the salt you lose through sweating.

Training instructors no longer force recruits to drink massive amounts of water, since too much water is as bad for you as too little. Instead, you'll be issued a canteen and you'll have plenty of opportunities to refill it. In most of the restrooms you'll find a urine color chart. The chart shows you what color your urine should be if you are well-hydrated. (An example can be found here: *http://www.nmcphc.med. navy.mil/downloads/healthyliv/nutrition/urinekleurenkaart.pdf.*)

Free Time

Free time is time when you can study, read your mail, write letters, take care of personal issues, etc. During free time there will be a training instructor on duty and you can consult with him or her, but he or she will not be leading any instruction. You have the right to one hour of free time per day on Mondays through Saturdays and roughly four hours on Sunday mornings and holidays, but you won't always get that full amount. It can be curtailed as a discipline or because you are out in the field or other because of other issues. Overall, though, you will get free time every day and if your flight has been especially good, your training instructor may be generous and give you two hours on a Saturday.

Graduation Requirements

In order to graduate from Air Force basic training, you must meet the following requirements:

- Participate in the BEAST
- Fire your service rifle
- Pass the final Physical Fitness Test (PFT)
- Pass the End of Course test
- Pass the individual drill progress check
- Attend all mandatory classes

Housing

Except during BEAST, recruits live in dorms, but unlike in college dorms, here you're sharing with a flight of men or women instead of just one roommate! You'll sleep in bunk beds, arranged head-to-feet, meaning the feet of recruit in the top bunk are above the head of the recruit in the bottom bunk. The recruits in the bunk beds on either side are arranged in the opposite way. This helps prevent the spread of disease. One of the very first things you will learn is how to make a bed the military way — and how to do it quickly. During BEAST, your accommodations will not be as grand. You will stay tents which you set up.

Each recruit has his or her own storage space in the dorm. Training instructors will teach you how to arrange your belongings in a military manner. You are expected to maintain your storage lockers and your belongings at all times. Recruits are responsible for cleaning the dorm, the bathrooms, and the training instructor's areas. Your training instructor will be very particular in how you keep your gear, looking at everything from the seams on your folded underwear to the corners of your bed, and even using the "white glove test" during inspections. (This is where an inspector, wearing white gloves, will swipe a finger over a part of your locker and then look to see if any dirt is left on his or her glove.)

All recruits have to work together to keep the dorm in top shape (Official U.S. Air Force photograph; Training Development Flight).

Hygiene

You are given time each day to take care of personal hygiene, but not a lot of time. You'll learn the fast, Air Force way of taking a shower, shaving, going to the bathroom, brushing your teeth, and getting dressed each morning. And you'll do it all in front of everyone in your dorm. There are no private bathrooms in basic training; showers and sinks are communal. But you'll be hurrying too much to worry about being shy.

Female recruits will not usually have enough time to shave their legs. Training instructors don't give you enough time on purpose; nicks and cuts on freshly shaved legs can quickly become infected by grime picked up during training. But most training instructors will give their recruits time to shave their legs before graduation or even on Saturday nights, if your flight has been meeting expectations.

There are portable bathrooms in the field and there are bathrooms in classroom areas, as well as in the dorm. Training instructors give recruits plenty of opportunities to use them, so you'll never need to worry about finding one when you need it. Female recruits may not get their periods during training because of the high level of activity and stress, but if they do, they simply carry supplies with them throughout the day. Supplies can be purchased at the Base Exchange as needed.

Male recruits have their heads shaved during Zero Week. They will visit the barbers each week for a trim. All of those haircuts are subtracted from their pay. Female recruits do not have their heads shaved, but they are expected to maintain neat and tidy hairstyles that keep the hair above the level of their collar. Women may have short hair, they may keep their hair in a bun, or they may have short, tight cornrows or similar styles. The important thing to remember is that any hairstyle you have must be able to be maintained neatly at all times, even when you are taking your helmet on and off, and there is not a lot of time at night for fixing complicated braids. (Something to keep in mind — if you have your hair in a bun, you are slightly more anonymous since that is how many female Airmen wear their hair. That can be good for staying below the radar.)

The combination of lots of people, high stress, and the sweat and dirt of training means that you have to be extra careful to remain healthy during basic training. Remember to wash your hands after using the restroom and before eating in order to prevent the spread of disease. Do not share combs, brushes, personal grooming tools, canteens, etc. with your fellow recruits. Make sure you work hard to keep the dorm as clean as possible.

Leadership Roles and Recruit Jobs

The Air Force wants recruits to begin learning and practicing leading immediately, so there are a number of leadership positions that recruits can volunteer for or be assigned to. Whether you must volunteer or if you will simply be assigned to a leadership role is up to the whim of the training instructor. The Air Force offers several recruit leadership positions:

- Dorm Chief: the Dorm Chief reports to the training instructor, helping him or her keep track of what is happening in the flight
- Element Leaders: each flight is divided up into several "elements" and each element has an Element Leader in charge of it; the Element Leaders report to the Dorm Chief

You should know, though, that being a leader during basic training does put you in the spotlight and that means that you will be more closely scrutinized by training instructors. It is not uncommon for recruit leaders to be disciplined when one of the recruits they are in charge of messes up or if the training instructor does not think that the recruiter leader has done a good job. Recruit leaders are often "fired" from their positions, but try not to take it personally. This is partially done to add to the stress of recruit training, but also to allow other recruits to have a chance to assume a leadership role.

There are also jobs which are given to specific recruits. These jobs include:

- Bed Aligners: these recruits make sure that all of the bunk beds are properly lined up in the sleeping area of the dorm
- Bowling Team: these are the recruits responsible for cleaning the bathrooms; the Bowling Team is led by the Latrine Queen
- Chow Runner: this is the recruit who announces your flight's entrance into the dining hall to the training instructors from other flights; this recruit also makes sure that each recruit in his or her flight knows where to sit in the dining hall
- Dayroom Team: these are the recruits who clean the dayroom; the dayroom is a large room in the dorm where the training instructor meets with the flight for discussion, mail call, and more
- Dorm Guard Monitor: this is the recruit that makes up the recruit guard schedule
- Guideon: this is the recruit who marches at the front of the flight and carries the flag

The Dorm Guard Monitor makes sure that someone is always standing guard at all hours of the day and night (Official U.S. Air Force photograph by Melinda Mueller).

- House Mouse: this is the recruit who runs errands for the training instructor
- Laundry Team: these are the recruits who are in charge of gathering dirty laundry, washing it, and returning it to its proper owners
- Road Guards: these recruits run at the front and back of the flight and stop traffic when the flight has to cross the road
- Shoe Aligners: these are the recruits who make sure that all of the shoes in the dorm are properly laid out under each bunk bed

Recycling or Getting Set Back

When you are recycled or set back in training, you are moved to another recruit training unit that is not as far along in training as the group you are currently assigned to. This can happen for a number of reasons. Sometimes it occurs for disciplinary reasons, because you have not followed instructions or have caused a serious violation. Other times recycling is done because you have not met the academic or physical standards that you need to in order to progress in training. If you fail an important test, then you can be set back to give you time to learn the skills you need to graduate. Recycling can also occur if you are injured or become seriously ill. For example, if you sprain your ankle during training, you will be given time to heal and then, because your training unit will have continued without you, you will be placed into a training unit that is at the same point in their training as you were when you were injured.

The Air Force has a special training program called the "Get Fit" program. Most of the recruits who head to "Get Fit" are recruits who do not pass the final physical fitness test taken in the seventh week of training, though recruits can be sent earlier if their training instructor feels they will not be able to be ready for the test. Recruits who are in the "Get Fit" program are otherwise on track to graduate, but they need extra physical training. They are given close attention by personal trainers to help them get ready to pass the test. If you are sent to the "Get Fit" program, you can stay in it for up to one month, but you are given a chance to retake the test sooner, in the hopes you will be able to rejoin your flight and graduate on time. Otherwise, time spent in the "Get Fit" program will delay your graduation date and affect your job placement and training.

Religious Services

Air Force recruits come from a wide variety of religious backgrounds and the Air Force tries hard to make sure that all of their recruits are able to practice their faith. During the time when your training instructor is getting to know his or her flight, you will be asked what religion you are. That will give them the information they need to plan for your religious needs. However, due to the demands of training, not all aspects of religious worship (such as Friday or Saturday services, special religious meals, or other religious requirements) may be able to be accommodated.

All religious services take place on Sunday mornings, regardless of the religion. The base chapel will offer at the very least a Catholic service and a Protestant Christian service. Recruits who are Jewish, Eastern Orthodox, Muslim, Pentecostal, Seventh-Day Adventist, Church of Christ, Christian Science, Latter-day Saints, Eckankar, Wicca, Baha'i, Buddhist, Hindu, and other religions will either attend services led by volunteers from the local community or by military religious personnel.

You are not required to attend religious services. If you do not currently practice any religion or if you are atheist, you can remain in the dorm during Sunday services. Or you are welcome to visit a different religious service each week to learn more about the faith. Some recruits attend services simply for the quiet and the break from training. On Sundays and during the week, Air Force chaplains are available to counsel recruits who are having trouble with some aspect of recruit training.

Safety, Injuries, and Illness

The personnel in charge of basic training are very careful to make it as safe as possible, even for a training regimen that involves live explosives! Training instructor training includes CPR, early detection of medical problems, suicide prevention, stress management, counseling techniques, and more. At every training location there are personnel to act as spotters and to assist recruits when needed. Medical personnel are on hand to treat injuries and illnesses and there are doctors and nurses stationed at the base hospital to treat more serious problems. Recruits are continually taught safety procedures, whether they are learning combat skills or learning how to fire their weapons. Accidents still do happen, but the vast majority of the time they are due to a recruit's error, not to negligence on the part of training personnel. Be sure you pay close attention to all safety briefings and that you follow all instructions to the letter.

If you get injured or get sick, you will be allowed to visit a doctor. He or she will determine how serious your injury or illness is. For less severe injuries or illnesses, the doctor may prescribe a day or two of light duty or bed rest. Your training instructors will be informed of this decision and will know how to take care of you. Follow any instructions given to you so that you can get back into training shape as quickly as possible. Returning to full training too soon could lead to further damage to your body, which could delay your training.

Recruits who are too injured or too sick to continue training with their flight are sent to the 319th Training Squadron. The 319th helps recruits heal from injuries, particularly ones involving muscles or bones, and recover from illness. (The 319th is also for recruits who may not be able to complete recruit training for reasons of serious injury, failing drug tests, or other issues.)

Days in the 319th do not count towards training. If you miss too many days, you will probably be dropped back to join another flight. Remember that this is for your safety and so that you have the opportunity to learn what you need to learn. Joining a new flight midway through training is hard, but learning how to adapt to a new situation and how to become part of a new team is part of military life.

Uniforms and Supplies

When you check in during Zero Week you will get your initial issue of clothing, gear, toiletries, and supplies. The initial issue covers everything from underwear to razor blades to running shoes to anything else you may need. You will also get a debit card which can be used at the Air Force Exchange to buy supplies and toiletries as you run out. During your time in basic training, you'll be issued even more gear and uniforms. Some of what you are issued, especially your uniform is yours; you are paying for it and you'll need it for the future. Other gear, such as your M16 rifle, is only yours during your time in basic training. It will be returned to supplies for the next recruit to use once you graduate.

Basic Training — Eight Weeks of Hard Work

Air Force basic training lasts for eight weeks and is broken into three phases, each of which is a different stage in a wartime deployment. The First Phase is Deployment Preparation. During Weeks One through Five, trainees learn the basic military skills necessary to head to war. The Second Phase is Deployment. Week Six is when trainees participate in the Basic Expeditionary Airman Skills Training, aka BEAST. This is a weeklong wartime deployment simulation run by recruits. The Third Phase is Reconstitution Time or returning from deployment. Weeks Seven and Eight are when trainees take their final tests, get ready to leave for job training, and, finally, graduate from basic military training.

Eight weeks sounds like a lot of time — and it is — but there are ways to help yourself see the time passing. Set short, medium, and long-term goals. The short term is easiest: give each day your best effort. For a medium goal, focus on getting through the week, learning as much as you can. Your longest term goal is obviously to graduate successfully, but you should also focus on the end of the current Phase. Each Phase has a specific focus, which will help you see your learning progression during that Phase. As you move through the Phases, you will begin to see how what you are learning all fits together.

Phase One or Deployment Preparation

By the end of Zero Week, you will be ready to begin Phase One or Deployment Preparation. While it may seem like you've already been in boot camp for almost a week — after all, you've been being yelled at and ordered about since you got to the reception building four days ago — this is when you start the classes that count towards graduation. From here on out you must complete the assignments, pass the tests, and learn the information presented to you over the next eight weeks or you will not graduate on time.

Deployment Preparation is focused on teaching you the basics of learning to be an Airman — how to fight, how to wear a uniform, how to handle and fire a weapon, how to maneuver, how the Air Force is organized, and how the Air Force expects you to behave. In order to teach you all of this information, the Air Force has specific topics it covers each week. Weeks one and two cover initial war skills; week three covers combat lifesaving; week four teaches you the basics of handling chemical, biological, radiological, nuclear, and enhanced/improved explosives (CBRNE) threats; and week five trains you to be a "ready warrior," an Airman who is prepared for deployment to a war-zone.

During weeks one and two, you have to learn the basics of being an Airman. You will take classes in Air Force history, learning about the battles the Air Force has fought in and the people who have led and shaped the Air Force. You will participate in discussions of the Air Force Core Values: Integrity First, Service Before Self, and Excellence in All We Do. Each of these values is discussed in depth individually over the course of basic training, both by classroom teachers and by your training instructors. There will be classroom courses on rank insignia, procedures for standing guard, dress and appearance, nutrition, career guidance, human relations, tactical movements, and more. At the end of week two, you will have your first dorm inspection.

The Air Force will issue you a weapon at the beginning of week one. This M-16 is identical to the ones used in the live fire training in week five, but it has been rendered inoperable so as to prevent accidents. (You will be able to tell the difference because the inoperable weapons have blue parts.) You will learn how to assemble and disassemble your weapon in under two minutes. You will also learn how to care for, store, clean, and carry your weapon, and you will learn to maintain your weapon at all times.

Starting at the beginning and continuing throughout basic training, you will be doing physical fitness six days a week. The Air Force has a graduated program designed to start you at one level of fitness and take you up to the level you need to achieve in order to meet graduation standards. To do this, your training instructor will lead you in one-hour long fitness workouts six days a week. Three of those days will focus on strength building (exercises like push-ups and sit-ups) and three of those days will focus on aerobic activity (such as running). You will also begin learning the basics of military drill, or marching in formation.

After learning basic skills the first two weeks of training, you'll then move onto more specialized training. Week three focuses on learning first aid. You will learn how to take care of yourself and your fellow Airmen, using skills to evaluate and field treat a variety of injuries, such

Recruits watch as their instructor explains an important first aid technique (Official U.S. Air Force photograph by Melinda Mueller).

as burns, spinal injuries, broken bones, internal bleeding, and more. The skills you learn in week three will be tested later on when you participate in BEAST.

Once you have learned the fundamentals of first aid, then you will start focusing on threat awareness. During week four you will learn about chemical, biological, radiological, nuclear, and enhanced explosives (CBRNE) threats. Your training will familiarize you with anti-terrorism activities, with cyberspace defense, with improvised explosive devices (IEDs), and with how to use your equipment to protect yourself in case of chemical or other attacks. As part of training, you will enter the CBRNE chamber, aka the gas chamber. The gas chamber is designed to show you how your gas mask works so that you will have confidence in its abilities should you need to use it during combat. The chamber also teaches you not to panic while in a chemical or other hazardous material situation. After instruction on using your mask, you will enter the chamber wearing your mask. CS Gas—a non-lethal gas used for riot control—will be released. You will have to take off your mask and repeat a series of information before you can leave the chamber. The gas will irritate your nose and throat, so you will cough and sneeze and your nose will run a *lot*. But remember not to panic—trust your equipment and trust your training—and know that the sensation will soon pass. You have to complete the gas chamber, so panicking will not help you. Recruits who don't complete will be sent back in as many times as needed until they do pass, so it is best to get it over with quickly the first time around!

Physical training will continue during weeks three and four. In addition to practicing your drills and participating in daily physical fitness exercises, you will also complete the Obstacle Course. The course is a mile and a half long and has seventeen different stations that you have to navigate. The Obstacle Course is designed to be a fun way to build your confidence in your physical abilities and get you over your fear of heights, water, and enclosed spaces. During week four you will also receive your second issue of clothing and you will be tested on assembly and disassembly of your weapon.

The goal of week five is to turn you into a warrior ready to leave for deployment in a few days. You will begin training to fight hand-to-hand, learning basic combative moves which are a mix of martial arts and combat sports. You'll learn how to keep your balance when attacked and how to protect yourself. Part of your warrior training is fighting with Pugil Sticks. Pugil Sticks look like oversized Q-Tips and they are designed to simulate combat with a bayonet, a blade that attaches to the front of a rifle. Recruits are paired off and try to use the sticks to knock each other out of the ring. It can look brutal, but it is a great way of working out aggression!

During week five, you will also practice other combat skills. You'll briefly trade in your non-operational M-16 for one that fires live rounds and you'll learn the proper way to sight your target, aim your weapon, and fire. You do not have to qualify with your weapon in order to graduate, but if you follow the instructions given you and practice carefully,

The Obstacle Course is designed to challenge you, but it can be fun also (Official U.S. Air Force photograph by Staff Sgt. Hillary Stonemetz).

Pugil stick fighting is all about aggression (Official U.S. Air Force photograph by Melinda Mueller).

you may shoot well enough to earn a marksmanship ribbon to wear on your uniform. Other classes, in preparation for combat, will focus on how to set up camp, how to prepare for and deal with the stresses of combat, basic leadership, basic situational awareness, handling public relations and the media, and more. At the end of week five, you will take your first written test, which covers everything you've learned so far. You will also undergo a physical fitness evaluation to make sure you are on track to pass the final physical fitness test at the end of week seven. Then you will be ready to head to BEAST.

Phase Two or Deployment

Deployment is designed to simulate a week of combat on the front lines. The formal name for it is Basic Expeditionary Airman Skills Training, but it is casually known as BEAST. BEAST takes place during five days in the middle of week six. It is designed to test recruits on all aspects of what they have learned so far during basic training, from first aid to weapons firing. Recruits are stressed physically and mentally, working on sleep which is regularly interrupted by 2 hour long guard duty sessions, while living in field conditions, meaning sleeping in tents and eating Meals-Ready-to-Eat (MREs) for two meals a day. These deprivations, along with heavy gear which must be worn at all times and a soundtrack of combat noises, are designed to simulate combat stresses and see how the recruits handle them. BEAST is also designed to test recruit's leadership and teamwork skills, so you will not be led by your military training instructor during BEAST. Instead, BEAST is run by the recruits themselves. There are training instructors on site to correct mistakes, play the "attacking forces," and insure safety, but you

BEAST is designed to simulate life during wartime deployment (Official U.S. Air Force photograph by Melinda Mueller).

and your fellow recruits are in charge of making sure your flight successfully completes BEAST.

BEAST starts with a four mile hike to the BEAST site. All day the first day, recruits will work with on-site instructors to set up camp and then go over basic skills one final time. There will be an official briefing, just as would occur during wartime. Early the next morning the "war" begins. There will be a wide variety of attacks—from conventional to improvised to chemical and biological—and missions—such as negotiating a combat obstacle course—spread out over the next four days. In between there is time for the instructors to go over mistakes and successes with your flight.

Each day will include time for physical fitness training, meals, and hygiene, but everything is secondary to the war simulation and any of those tasks may be interrupted by announcements of incoming forces or aerial attacks. Part of the challenge of the BEAST is that as the hours pass, recruits become very tired and hungry, making it more difficult to work together. The Air Force wants you to be able to operate under these conditions. The instructors on site will act as mentors during BEAST, helping you remember your training and making sure you remember to stay focused on teamwork, but the combat simulations are in your hands and the hands of your fellow recruits. Some recruits will be assigned as student leaders, in charge of operations within their zone and in charge of scheduling the recruits under their command for time standing guard and manning defensive firing positions. Your job is to learn to think for yourself, to work with your teammates, and to accept responsibility for your actions during the exercises.

After four days of simulated combat, the "war" is declared over. On Friday of week six, you will start the day with a Victory Breakfast, celebrating your flight's completion of BEAST. Afterwards, there will be a presentation of any awards that recruits and/or flights may have earned during BEAST, then you will break down camp and head back to your dorm and your training instructors. You will be given time to do some much needed laundry and take showers and then you'll start

learning the Air Force post-deployment — or reconstitution — procedures.

Phase Three or Reconstitution Time (Post-Deployment)

Reconstitution time is designed to simulate the time when Airmen
return from deployment. During week seven, the first week of Reconstitution, the Air Force evaluates recruits to make sure they have learned
the military skills they need to learn in order to graduate and that they
know the basic Airmanship skills they will need once they enter active
or reserve duty. There will still be classroom lessons, covering recovery
from combat stress, financial planning, ethics, military history, sexual
assault prevention, environmental awareness, etc. You will have to pass
the final Physical Fitness Test (PFT):

Event	Final PFT Minimum — Men
Run	1.5 mile run in 11 min. 57 sec.
Push-ups (in 2 min.)	33
Sit-ups (in 2 min.)	42

Event	Final PFT Minimum — Women
Run	1.5 mile run in 14 min. 26 sec.
Push-ups (in 2 min.)	18
Sit-ups (in 2 min.)	38

Even though this evaluation takes place in week seven, if you do
not pass it, but you are otherwise on track to graduate, you will be sent
to the "Get Fit" program to get into better shape. If you do not pass it
and you are also lacking in other skills, then you will likely be recycled,
meaning set back to another flight that is at an earlier stage of training,
and you will not graduate with the rest of your flight.

Week eight is your last week at basic training, but you can't slack
off now. You still have to take your final written test, which covers
everything you've learned throughout basic training and which must

Your last test covers all of the topics you learned throughout basic military training (Official U.S. Air Force photograph by Melinda Mueller).

be passed in order to graduate. In addition to the test, you will attend briefings which will remind you of the core values and how to uphold them, prepare you for technical school (job) training, and teach you how to behave as an Airman while out on a town pass. Soon it will be time for graduation and you will be a full-fledged Airman!

Graduation and Beyond

Most of the last few days of Air Force Basic Military Training revolve around getting ready for graduation. New Airmen turn in the gear that they aren't keeping and pick up the personal effects they dropped off when they arrived weeks previously. Dorms are straightened, men get haircuts, and there is a rehearsal for graduation.

Airman's Run, Airman's Coin Ceremony, and On-Base Liberty

Thursday of week eight is the first day of graduation. The day starts with the Airman's Run, a mile-and-a-half run through the middle of base, starting at 8 A.M. Your family and friends will line up on either side of the route and cheer you on. Afterwards, you will be given time to clean up and then you will head to the Airman's Coin Ceremony, the official graduation ceremony.

The Coin Ceremony is a proud moment. Recruits who have distinguished themselves in various ways will be recognized, as will any visiting dignitaries. There are a few tips to help make the day more enjoyable:

- *Don't make travel plans too early.* Your family should not make arrangements until you alert them to do so. There are a lot of things that can delay your training and they won't want to have to try to change plane tickets or hotel reservations if your graduation day changes. You will have arranged your own final travel details during recruit training, so you will have a way to get to get to your next phase of training.

- *Dress for the weather.* San Antonio can be very hot and sunny, especially during the summer. Remind your family to bring sunscreen, sunglasses, hats, and other protection, as well as water bottles so they do not get dehydrated. But during the winter, San Antonio can be chilly in the mornings, so it is important that they remember to bring jackets and/or sweaters. If it is raining, the Coin Ceremony will be moved indoors.
- *Dress appropriately.* Families can either dress up for the ceremony, just as they would for a high school or college graduation, or they may choose to wear shirts with your flight information on it. Either is appropriate and acceptable.
- *Bring something to occupy small children.* The Coin Ceremony is

A new Airman receives her Airman's Coin from her training instructor (Official U.S. Air Force photograph).

not long, but it can be too dry for small children. Bring books or small, quiet toys to keep them occupied.

If your family cannot come to graduation because of financial reasons, there are often groups who might be able to help. Check with your house of worship or local Air Force reserve unit to see if they might have a program to assist families in attending graduation.

Once the Coin Ceremony is over, you will be given liberty — time off — to spend with your friends and family on base. A few tips for a successful on-base liberty:

- Your training instructors will give you clear instructions for how you are to behave. Follow these instructions to the letter. Return on time at the end of the day. *DO NOT* mess up. Until you leave for your technical school on Monday, you can still be sent back to start training over.
- Arrive early. Remind your family that they will have to check in on base in order to be allowed to visit, so they need to allow time for that.
- Obey all traffic laws. Speed limits on base are often very slow, usually 20–35 miles per hour. The Air Force takes these speed limits very seriously and your family will be pulled over if they violate them.
- Don't overeat. You'll be able to get food from wherever you like on base, but your stomach will not be used to soda and sweets and other junk food after so many weeks of doing without. You don't want to make yourself sick.
- Take time to sit and catch up. You'll want to show your family around base, but take some time to just sit quietly and talk. It will be the first time you've been able to see them in several months and you'll want to hear how they've been.
- Include fellow Airmen whose families cannot come. There will probably be at least one member of your flight whose family cannot make it to graduation. Include him or her as a part of your family — after all, you are both Airmen now.

Graduation Parade and Town Pass

On Friday, at 9 A.M., there will be a Graduation Parade, which will allow you and your fellow graduates to show off your marching and drill. Your family will want to arrive on base as early as 7:15 in order to catch a bus to the Parade Grounds. After the parade is over, you will have the opportunity to show your family around your dormitory and introduce them to your training instructor. At 11:15 A.M., all graduates are given a town pass, allowing them to leave with their families to visit San Antonio. Be sure to follow the instructions of your training instructor and to read over the suggestions for on-base liberty behavior. Messing up now could still result in you being recycled back to another flight to retake a portion of training.

On Saturday, you will also be given a town pass, provided you

The Graduation Parade allows new Airmen to show their skills and discipline off to their loved ones (Official U.S. Air Force photograph by Melinda Mueller).

have behaved properly and your training instructor hasn't taken it away from you for any reason. You will still have to stay in San Antonio, but you'll have the entire day to spend with your family. Sunday morning your family can meet you on base to attend religious services with you. All graduates will have on-base liberty on Sunday, but Honor graduates, Airmen in Honor flights, and those Airmen who were recognized for being the most physically fit will receive another off-base town pass.

After Graduation

And now you are an Airman. Congratulations! But your journey has just begun. You still have more training to go through before you'll actually begin doing the job you signed on to do. You will have to be back on base Sunday night to prepare to leave for technical training. You will travel to technical training on the Monday following Graduation activities. You will not receive any leave time (vacation) until after your job training course is over. Training at technical schools can last from a month to over a year, depending upon what your Military Occupational Specialty is. From there you'll be sent to your first permanent duty station and begin your career as an Airman.

Glossary of Military Terms

Active Duty— those military personnel who serve full time

AFQT: The Armed Forces Qualifying Test— a part of the ASVAB; made up of four tests that measure your knowledge of math and language skills; the AFQT used to determine your eligibility for military enlistment

Air Force— the branch of the military responsible for air warfare

Allowances— moneys which help military personnel pay for housing, food, uniforms, etc.

Army— the branch of the military responsible for land warfare

ASVAB: the Armed Services Vocational Aptitude Battery— a series of tests taken to determine your skills and knowledge; used for job placement in the military

Barracks— dormitory style housing on military bases

Basic Training or Recruit Training (also called Boot Camp)— the initial training for new enlisted military personnel; lasts between seven and thirteen weeks depending upon the branch of the service

CAST: Computer Adaptive Screening Test or *EST: Enlistment Screening Test*— a mini–ASVAB test taken in a recruiter's office which shows what a potential enlistee's AFQT score will probably be; used to help potential enlistees know if their scores will qualify them for enlistment

CAT: Computer Adaptive Test— name of the ASVAB test when taken on computer

Chaplain— the military term for a religious leader, preacher, minister, rabbi, imam, etc.

Civilians— those persons not serving in the military

Coast Guard— the branch of the military responsible for law enforcement on the waters (lakes, rivers, etc.) in and around the United States

Commissary— a grocery store on a military base

Conscientious Objector— someone who refuses to fight or participate in any war because of religious, personal, moral, or ethical beliefs

DEP: Delayed Entry Program— the period of time between finalizing the enlistment process and leaving for basic training; length varies from a few weeks to 365 days

Dependents— any people that a military person has to take care of: a spouse, any children or stepchildren living in the home who are under 18 and unmarried, and any other family members who rely on a military member for more than half of their support

DoD: Department of Defense— the government agency that oversees four branches of the military — Air Force, Army, Navy, Marines; the Coast Guard is under the Department of Homeland Security

Don't Ask, Don't Tell— a policy put in place in 1993 which allowed homosexuals to serve in the military, but only if they did not tell anyone their sexual orientation or participate in homosexual activities (i.e., sex or gay marriage); overturned in December 2010; fully repealed in September 2011

Enlisted— those military personnel who are responsible for the daily operations of the military under the command of officers; ranks range from E-1 to E-9

Enlistment Process— the steps taken to join the military as an enlisted person

Exchange— a department or general goods store on a military base

Incentive Pay— special pay which some military personnel earn because of the job they do or the risks to which they are exposed

IRR: Individual Ready Reserve— former military personnel who do not drill or receive pay, but who can still be called up to active duty; the last years of an enlistment are spent in the IRR

Marine Corps— the branch of the military responsible for amphibious (sea-to-land) warfare

MEPS: Military Entrance Processing Station— a Department of Defense facility that is in charge of physical and mental exams of potential enlistees, as well as administering the Oath of Enlistment and shipping new recruits off to basic training

MET: Mobile Examining Team— a facility that exists solely to administer the ASVAB test to potential enlistees

Military Training Instructor— the Air Force term for the person in charge of recruits during recruit training

MOS: Military Occupational Specialty— the job field you will be assigned and trained in

MRE: Meal-Ready-to-Eat— portable, long-lasting, prepackaged meal eaten during field maneuvers and combat

National Guard— the reserve military programs that are managed by individual states, rather than by the Federal Government; there are two: Army National Guard and Air National Guard (Air Force)

Navy— the branch of the military responsible for warfare on the sea

NCOs: Non-commissioned officers— the upper enlisted ranks; NCOs act as leaders and managers; generally the ranks of E-4 to E-9, with E-4 to E-6 called junior NCOs and E-7 to E-9 called senior NCOs

Oath of Enlistment— the official swearing-in pledge that all new recruits take just before leaving for basic training

Officers— the command personnel of the military branches; ranks range from O-1 to O-9

PAP: Paper and Pencil— name of the ASVAB test taken on paper

Pay grade— the level of pay a particular military member is eligible for each month

Post–9/11 GI Bill— the most commonly used education program for all branches of the military; it provides money for tuition and other expenses

Rank— the position you hold within the military; can be enlisted, warrant officer, or officer

Recruiter— the military man or woman who is responsible for giving out information about joining the military, finding candidates for enlistment, checking their qualifications, guiding them through the enlistment process, and offering tips on how to prepare for recruit training

Reserves— those military personnel who serve part-time, training one weekend a month and two weeks a year; they can be called up to active duty when needed

Stop Loss— a program which allows the military, during times of conflict, to prevent personnel from leaving the military on their normal separation date for up to one year; used during times of war to keep needed personnel on active duty

Technical Subtests— a part of the ASVAB; made up of five tests that measure your knowledge of and aptitude (natural talent) for technical skills; the technical subtests are used to determine which jobs you are eligible for

Tricare— the military's health care plan

UCMJ: Uniform Code of Military Justice— the official military laws of the United States, parts of which cover the criminal prosecution of military personnel

USO: United Services Organizations, Inc.— a private, nonprofit group that support military personnel by providing morale, welfare, and recreational services

Waiver— official approval that allows someone to enlist in the military despite not meeting a particular qualification or qualifications

Warrant Officers— a specialty rank that falls in-between enlisted personnel and officers; the Air Force is the only branch that does not have Warrant Officers

For More Information

Further Information about the Air Force and the United States Military

BOOKS

Axelrod, Alan. *Encyclopedia of the U.S. Air Force*. New York: Checkmark, 2006.

Boyne, Walter J. *Beyond the Wild Blue: A History of the United States Air Force, 1947–2007*. 2nd edition. New York: Thomas Dunne, 2007.

A Day in the Life of the United States Armed Forces. New York: Epicom Media, 2003.

Dolan, Edward F. *Careers in the U.S. Air Force*. Military Service. New York: Marshall Cavendish/Benchmark, 2010.

Schading, Barbara. *A Civilian's Guide to the U.S. Military: A Comprehensive Reference to the Customs, Language, and Structure of the Armed Forces*. Cincinnati, OH: Writer's Digest, 2007.

Tillman, Barrett. *Alpha Bravo Delta Guide to the U.S. Air Force*. Walter J. Boyne, series editor. Indianapolis, IN: Alpha, 2003.

VIDEOS

Inside Today's Military: *http://www.todaysmilitary.com/inside*.

Videos on the Air Force's Recruiting Site: *http://www.airforce.com/see-what-its-like*.

WEBSITES

United States Air Force's Offical Site: *http://www.af.mil*.

Department of Defense's Official Site: *http://www.defense.gov*.

About.com's U.S. Military site: *http://usmilitary.about.com*.

Military.com: *http://www.military.com*. [NOTE: To access some information on Military.com, you will have to register and your information will be shared with recruiters.]

Military Woman: *http://www.militarywoman.org.*

Today's Military: *http://www.todaysmilitary.com.*

Military Career Planning

BOOKS

Careers in Focus: Armed Forces. New York: Ferguson, 2008.

Goldberg, Jan. *Careers for Patriotic Types and Others Who Want to Serve Their Country.* Careers for You. 2nd edition. New York: McGraw-Hill, 2006.

Henderson, C.J., and Jack Dolphin. *Career Opportunities in the Armed Forces.* 2nd edition. Revised by Pamela Fehl. New York: Ferguson, 2007.

150 Best Jobs Through Military Training. Indianapolis, IN: JIST, 2008.

Sterngass, Jon. *Armed Forces.* Great Careers with a High School Diploma. New York: Ferguson, 2008.

WEBSITES

ASVAB Career Exploration Program: *http://www.asvabprogram.com.*

Military Career Information: *http://usmilitary.about.com/od/theorderlyroom/u/career_info.htm.*

Military Careers: *http://www.todaysmilitary.com/careers.*

My Future: *http://www.myfuture.com.* [This is a Department of Defense website that brings together information about careers, colleges, and military service provided by the Departments of Commerce, Defense, Education and Labor.]

Military Benefits

BOOK

Michel, Christopher P., and Terry Howell. *The Military Advantage: The Military.com Guide to Military and Veterans Benefits.* 2010 edition. Annapolis, MD: Naval Institute Press, 2010.

WEBSITES

Defense Finance and Accounting Service — Military Pay: *http://www.dfas.mil/militarypay.html.*

Department of Veterans Affairs' GI Bill Site: *http://www.gibill.va.gov.*

Department of Veterans Affairs' Jack-of-All-Trades page: *http://www.gibill. va.gov/bill-of-all-trades/index.html.* [Gives information on non-college programs that are supported by the GI Bill.]

Department of Veterans Affairs' WEAMS Institution Search: *http://inquiry. vba.va.gov/weamspub/buildSearchInstitutionCriteria.do.* [Allows you to search for continuing education programs which will be covered by the GI Bill.]

Military Benefits: *http://www.military.com/Benefits.*

Military Benefits: *http://www.myfuture.com/military/articles-advice/military-benefits.*

Military Pay and Benefits: *http://usmilitary.about.com/od/militarypay/u/pay_ and_benefits.htm.*

So Much More Than Just a Paycheck: *http://www.todaysmilitary.com/benefits.*

Understanding the Post-9/11 GI Bill: *http://images.military.com/media/ education/pdf/post911_gibill.pdf.*

Enlistment Information

BOOK

Ostrow, Scott. *Guide to Joining the Military.* 2nd edition. Lawrenceville, NJ: ARCO, 2003.

VIDEO

A Day at the MEPS: *http://www.mepcom.army.mil/video.html.*

WEBSITES

U.S. Air Force's Official Recruiting Site: *http://www.airforce.com.*

10 Steps to Joining the Military: *http://www.military.com/Recruiting.*

Joining the Military: *http://usmilitary.about.com/od/joiningthemilitary/u/ joining_up.htm.*

Air Force Recruiting Service

Use this contact information to report inappropriate behavior on the part of a recruiter.

Website: http://www.rs.af.mil/main/contactus.asp

Telephone: Air Force Recruiting Service Public Affairs: (210) 565–4687 (tell them what your situation is and ask them to direct you to someone in the chain of command)

ASVAB: Information and Study Guides

BOOKS

Ostrow, Scott A. *Master the ASVAB.* 21st ed. Lawrenceville, NJ: Thomson/ Arco, 2008. [Includes information on military careers.]

Powers, Rod. *ASVAB AFQT for Dummies.* Hoboken, NJ: Wiley, 2010.

_____, and Jennifer Lawler. *ASVAB for Dummies.* 2nd ed. Hoboken, NJ: Wiley, 2007. [Includes information on which subtests correspond to which military job.]

Stradley, Laura, and Robin Kavanagh. *The Complete Idiot's Guide to the ASVAB: Time-Tested Techniques for Acing the ASVAB!* New York: Alpha, 2010.

WEBSITES

ASVAB Career Exploration Program: *http://www.asvabprogram.com.*

ASVAB's Official Site: *http://www.official-asvab.com.*

March2Success: *https://www.march2success.com.* [A test-prep site developed by the U.S. Army.]

Life During Air Force Recruit Training

BOOKS

Nicolls, MSgt. Boone, USAF (Ret.). *Airman's Guide.* 7th edition. Mechanicsburg, PA: Stackpole, 2007. [This contains the information you will learn in basic training and more.]

Powers, Rod. *Basic Training for Dummies.* Hoboken, NJ: Wiley, 2011.

Van Wormer, SrA Nicholas. *The Ultimate Air Force Basic Training Guidebook: Tips, Tricks, and Tactics for Surviving Boot Camp.* New York: Savas Beatie, 2010.

VIDEOS

Basic Military Training: *http://www.airforce.com/joining-the-air-force/basic-military-training.*

Recruit Travel Video: *http://www.mepcom.army.mil/travel-video.html.* [Tells new recruits the procedures that should be followed while traveling to basic training.]

WEBSITES

737th Training Group, AF Basic Military Training, Lackland Air Force Base: *http://www.basictraining.af.mil.*

What to Expect Factsheet: *http://www.basictraining.af.mil/library/factsheets/ factsheet.asp?id=15717.*

Books for Younger Readers

Demarest, Chris L. *Alpha Bravo Charlie: The Military Alphabet.* New York: Margaret K. McElderry Books, 2005.

Donovan, Sandy. *The U.S. Air Force.* U.S. Armed Forces. Minneapolis, MN: Lerner, 2005.

Goldish, Meish. *Air Force: Civilian to Airman.* Becoming a Soldier. New York: Bearport, 2011.

Hamilton, John. *The Air Force.* Defending the Nation. Edina, MN: Abdo, 2007.

Resources

Allison, Aimee, and David Solnit. *Army of None: Strategies to Counter Military Recruitment, End War, and Build a Better World.* New York: Seven Stories Press, 2007.

American Women and the United States Armed Forces: A Guide to the Records of Military Agencies in the National Archives Relating to American Women. Compiled by Charlotte Palmer Seeley. Revised by Virginia C. Purdy and Robert Gruber. Washington, DC: National Archives and Records Administration, 1992.

Ashabranner, Brent. *A Date with Destiny: The Women in Military Service for America Memorial.* Photographs by Jennifer Ashabranner. Great American Memorials series. Brookfield, CT: Twenty-first Century Books, 2000.

Axelrod, Alan. *Encyclopedia of the U.S. Air Force.* New York: Checkmark, 2006.

Baker, Anni. *Life in the U.S. Armed Forces: (Not) Just Another Job.* Westport, CT: Praeger Security International, 2008.

Bradford, James C., ed. *International Encyclopedia of Military History.* New York: Routledge, 2006.

Buckley, Gail. *American Patriots: The Story of Blacks in the Military from the Revolution to Desert Storm.* Adapted by Tonya Bolden. New York: Crown, 2003.

Burns, Robert. "Ask and Tell: 18-Year Ban of Gays in Military Is Lifted." *Charlotte Observer,* September 21, 2011, sec. A.

_____. "Military Is 'Adequately Prepared' to End Ban on Gays, Says Pentagon." *Charlotte Observer,* September 20, 2011, sec. A.

Careers in Focus: Armed Forces. New York: Ferguson, 2008.

Chambers, John Whiteclay II, ed. *The Oxford Companion to American Military History.* New York: Oxford University Press, 1999.

Collins, Robert F. *Basic Training: What to Expect and How to Prepare.* Military Opportunity. New York: Rosen, 1988.

Cooper, Jason. *U. S. Marine Corps*. Fighting Forces. Vero Beach, FL: Rourke, 2004.

Defense Finance and Accounting Service. "Military Pay Tables—1949 to 2011." http://www.dfas.mil/militarymembers/payentitlements/military paytables.html.

Department of Defense. *Personnel & Procurement Reports and Data Files*. DoD Personnel & Procurement Statistics. http://siadapp.dmdc.osd. mil.

Dillon, C. Hall. "The Military Offers Valuable Training for Civilian Careers." In *Choosing a Career*, edited by Linda Aksomitis. Issues That Concern You. Detroit: Gale, 2008.

Dolan, Edward F. *Careers in the U.S. Air Force*. Military Service. New York: Marshall Cavendish/Benchmark, 2010.

Donovan, Sandy. *The U.S. Air Force*. U.S. Armed Forces. Minneapolis, MN: Lerner, 2005.

Doubler, Michael D. *The National Guard and Reserve: A Reference Handbook*. Contemporary Military, Strategic, and Security Issues. Westport, CT: Praeger Security International, 2008.

Dribben, Melissa. "Sexual Assault a Silent Battle for Servicewomen." *Charlotte Observer*, September 18, 2011, sec. A.

Gay, Kathlyn. *The Military and Teens: The Ultimate Teen Guide*. It Happened to Me, No. 21. Lanham, MD: Scarecrow, 2008.

Gibbs, Nancy. "Sexual Assaults on Female Soldiers: Don't Ask, Don't Tell." *Time,* March 8, 2010. http://www.time.com/time/magazine/article/0,91 71,1968110,00.html.

Goldberg, Jan. *Careers for Patriotic Types and Others Who Want to Serve Their Country*. Careers for You. 2nd ed. New York: McGraw-Hill, 2006.

Goldstein, Joshua S. *War and Gender: How Gender Shapes the War System and Vice Versa*. Cambridge: Cambridge University Press, 2001.

Hamilton, John. *The Air Force*. Defending the Nation. Edina, MN: Abdo, 2007.

Harris, Bill. *The Complete Idiot's Guide to Careers in the Military*. Indianapolis, IN: Alpha, 2002.

Hearn, Chester G. *Air Force: An Illustrated History—The U.S. Air Force from the 1910s to the 21st Century*. Minneapolis, MN: Zenith, 2008.

Henderson, C.J., and Jack Dolphin. *Career Opportunities in the Armed Forces*. 2nd ed. Revised by Pamela Fehl. New York: Ferguson, 2007.

Herbert, Don. *63 Days and a Wake-Up: Your Survival Guide to United States Army Basic Combat Training*. New York: iUniverse, 2007.

Kilpatrick, Kelly. "Things to Consider Before Joining the US Military." *US Military*. About.com. http://usmilitary.about.com/od/joiningthemilitary/a/consider.htm.

Lande, David A. "Saved by the Wild Blue Yonder." *Air Force Times,* September 2010. http://www.airforce-magazine.com/MagazineArchive/Pages/2010/September%202010/0910song.aspx.

Leff, Lisa. "Active-Duty Gays: Coming Out Has Been Nonevent." *Army Times,* October 16, 2011. http://www.armytimes.com/news/2011/10/ap-military-dont-ask-dont-tell-gays-coming-out-nonevent-101611.

Michel, Christopher P., and Terry Howell. *The Military Advantage: The Military.com Guide to Military and Veterans Benefits.* 2010 ed. Annapolis, MD: Naval Institute Press, 2010.

Military.com. "Learn to Use Your GI Bill Benefits." *Education.* http://www.military.com/education/content/gi-bill/learn-to-use-your-gi-bill.html.

_____. "Military Benefits." *Benefits.* http://www.military.com/Benefits.

Nathan, Amy. *Count on Us: American Women in the Military.* Washington, DC: National Geographic Society, 2004.

National Aeronautics and Space Administration. "Jacqueline 'Jackie' Cochran." *United States Centennial of Flight Commission.* http://www.centennialofflight.gov/essay/Explorers_Record_Setters_and_Daredevils/cochran/EX25.htm. 2003.

Nicolls, MSgt. Boone, USAF (Ret.). *Airman's Guide.* 7th edition. Mechanicsburg, PA: Stackpole, 2007.

Ordoñez, Franco. "Military Gets Ready for a New Era." *Charlotte Observer,* August 28, 2011, sec. A.

Ostrow, Scott A. *Guide to Joining the Military.* 2nd ed. Lawrenceville, NJ: Thomson/Arco, 2004.

_____. *Master the ASVAB.* 21st ed. Lawrenceville, NJ: Thomson/Arco, 2008.

Paradis, Adrian A. *Opportunities in Military Careers.* Rev. ed. New York: McGraw-Hill, 2006.

Parker, Ashley. "Lawsuit Says Military Is Rife with Sexual Abuse." The *New York Times,* February 15, 2011. http://www.nytimes.com/2011/02/16/us/16military.html.

Philpott, Tom. "Gay Benefits Rules Drafted." *Headlines.* Military.com, December 2, 2010. http://www.military.com/features/0,15240,223455,00.html.

Porterfield, Jason. *Frequently Asked Questions About College and Career Training.* Teen Life. New York: Rosen, 2009.

Powers, Rod. *US Military.* About.com. http://usmilitary.about.com.

_____, and Jennifer Lawler. *ASVAB for Dummies.* 2nd ed. Hoboken, NJ: Wiley, 2007.

Rosen, James. "First Lady to Visit Army Base in S.C." *Charlotte Observer,* January 24, 2011, sec. A.

Schading, Barbara. *A Civilian's Guide to the U.S. Military: A Comprehensive Reference to the Customs, Language, and Structure of the Armed Forces.* Cincinnati, OH: Writer's Digest Books, 2007.

Stalsburg, Brittany L. "After Repeal: LGBT Service Members and Veterans: The Facts." *Publications.* Service Women's Action Network, 2011. http://servicewomen.org/wp-content/uploads/2011/10/LGBT-Fact-Sheet-09 1411.pdf.

_____. "Rape, Sexual Assault and Sexual Harassment in the Military: The Quick Facts." *Publications.* Service Women's Action Network, 2011. http://servicewomen.org/wp-content/uploads/2011/09/R-SASH-Quick-Facts-08 1811.pdf.

Stewart, Gail B. *Fighting for Freedom: Blacks in the American Military.* Lucent Library of Black History. Detroit, MI: Thompson Gale, 2006.

Stradley, Laura, and Robin Kavanagh. *The Complete Idiot's Guide to the ASVAB: Time-Tested Techniques for Acing the ASVAB!* New York: Alpha, 2010.

Tate, Curtis. "Pentagon Lets Chaplains Perform Gay Weddings." The *Charlotte Observer,* October 1, 2011, sec. A.

Thompson, Peter. *The Real Insider's Guide to Military Basic Training: A Recruit's Guide of Important Secrets and Hints to Successfully Complete Boot Camp.* Rev. ed. Universal Publishers/uPUBLISH.com, 2002.

Thompson, Wayne. "Air Force, United States: History." *World Book Encyclopedia.* 2003 ed.

Tillman, Barrett. *Alpha Bravo Delta Guide to the U.S. Air Force.* Walter J. Boyne, series editor. Indianapolis, IN: Alpha, 2003.

Understanding the Post-9/11 GI Bill. Military Advantage, 2009. http://images.military.com/media/education/pdf/post-911-gi-bill.pdf.

United States Air Force. *Official Site.* http://www.af.mil.

_____. *Recruiting Web Site.* http://www.airforce.com.

United States Army. "Symbols & Insignias." *Official Site.* http://www.army.mil/symbols.

United States Census Bureau. *Statistical Abstract.* http://www.census.gov/compendia/statab.

United States Department of Veterans Affairs. *GI Bill Web Site.* http://www.gibill.va.gov/.

United States Federal Government. "U.S. Code TITLE 10 > Subtitle C >

PART I > CHAPTER 31 > § 502. Enlistment Oath: Who May Administer." *Legal Information Institute.* Cornell University Law School. http://www.law.cornell.edu/uscode/html/uscode10/usc_sec_10_00000502----000-.html.

United States Military Entrance Processing Command. *Enlistment Processing.* http://www.mepcom.army.mil/enlistment.html.

_____. *USMEPCOM Videos.* http://www.mepcom.army.mil/MEPCOM_videos.html.

Van Wormer, SrA Nicholas. *The Ultimate Air Force Basic Training Guidebook: Tips, Tricks, and Tactics for Surviving Boot Camp.* New York: Savas Beatie, 2010.

Vaughn, Kirby Lee. *The Enlistment Planning Guide: How to Make the Most of Your Military Service.* Santa Barbara, CA: Essayons, 1995.

Volkin, Sergeant Michael. *The Ultimate Basic Training Guidebook: Tips, Tricks, and Tactics for Surviving Boot Camp.* 4th ed. New York: Savas Beatie, 2009.

Watson, Cynthia A. *U.S. Military Service: A Reference Handbook.* Contemporary World Issues. Santa Barbara, CA: ABC-CLIO, 2007.

Watson, Julie. "For Gay Troops, Changes Precede End of DADT." *Marine Corps Times,* September 18, 2011. http://www.marinecorpstimes.com/news/2011/09/ap-for-gay-troops-changes-precede-end-of-dadt-091811.

Weill-Greenberg, Elizabeth, ed. *10 Excellent Reasons Not to Join the Military.* New York: The New Press, 2006.

Wings Across America. "WASP Facts." *WASP on the Web.* http://www.wingsacrossamerica.us/wasp/facts.htm.

Women in Military Service for America Memorial Foundation, Inc. "Statistics on Women in the Military." *For the Press.* http://www.womensmemorial.org/PDFs/StatsonWIM.pdf.

Youssef, Nancy A. "Military Outlines New Policy on Gays." *Charlotte Observer,* January 29, 2011, sec. A.

Index

Numbers in **_bold italics_** indicate pages with photographs.